CAROL ANN DUFFY lives in Manchester, where she is
Professor and Creative Director of the Writing School at
Manchester Metropolitan University. She has written for both
children and adults, and her poetry has received many awards,
including the Signal Prize for Children's Verse, the Whitbread
and Forward Prizes, and the Lannan and E. M. Forster Prize in
America. In 2005, she won the T. S. Eliot Prize for *Rapture*.
She was appointed Poet Laureate in 2009.

CAROL ANN DUFFY

New Selected Poems

1984–2004

PICADOR

First published 2004 by Picador

This revised paperback edition published 2011 by Picador
an imprint of Pan Macmillan, a division of Macmillan Publishers Limited
Pan Macmillan, 20 New Wharf Road, London N1 9RR
Basingstoke and Oxford
Associated companies throughout the world
www.panmacmillan.com

ISBN 978-1-4472-0642-2

1 3 5 7 9 8 6 4 2

A CIP catalogue record for this book is available from
the British Library.

'Are You Lonesome Tonight', words by Roy Turk and Lou Handman, © 1926 by
Bourne & Co. All rights reserved – lyric reproduced by kind permission of Redwood Music Ltd
(Carlin), London NW1 8BD. 'These Boots Are Made for Walking', words and music by Lee Hazelwood,
copyright © 1964 Criterion Music Corp., copyright renewed, copyright © 1993 Criterion Music Corp.
All rights reserved for Criterion Music Corp., administered in the UK and Eire by
Marada Music Ltd. Used by kind permission of Criterion Music Corp.

Every effort has been made to contact copyright holders of material reproduced
in this book. If any have been inadvertently overlooked, the publishers
will be pleased to make restitution at the earliest opportunity.

Printed in the UK by CPI Mackays, Chatham ME5 8TD

Visit www.picador.com to read more about all our books
and to buy them. You will also find features, author interviews and
news of any author events, and you can sign up for e-newsletters
so that you're always first to hear about our new releases.

For Ella

Acknowledgements

Thanks and acknowledgements are due to
Anvil Press Poetry, Faber and Faber, Picador,
and to all the publications which first published these poems.

Also to the many organizers of
poetry readings and festivals in the UK and Ireland,
particularly Helen Taylor, Maura Dooley, Theo Dorgan,
Michael Woods, Tony Ellis, Bob Mole, Barry and Tricia Wood,
Jane Thomas, John Osborne, Catherine Lockerbie
and (a special thanks) Simon Powell.

Carol Ann Duffy is grateful for a NESTA Fellowship.

Contents

from Selling Manhattan

from The Other Country

Other Poems

from The World's Wife

from **Feminine Gospels**

from Standing Female Nude

(1985)

Girl Talking

On our Eid day my cousin was sent to
the village. Something happened. We think it was pain.
She gave wheat to the miller and the miller
gave her flour. Afterwards it did not hurt,
so for a while she made chapattis. *Tasleen,*
said her friends, *Tasleen, do come out with us.*

They were in a coy near the swing. It's like
a field. Sometimes we planted melons, spinach,
marrow, and there was a well. She sat on the swing.
They pushed her till she shouted, *Stop the swing,*
then she was sick. Tasleen told them to find
help. She made blood beneath the mango tree.

Her mother held her down. She thought something
was burning her stomach. We paint our hands.
We visit. We take each other money.
Outside, the children played Jack-with-Five-Stones.
Each day she'd carried water from the well
into the Mosque. Men washed and prayed to God.

After an hour she died. Her mother cried.
They called a Holy Man. He walked from Dina
to Jhang Chak. He saw her dead, then said,
She went out at noon and the ghost took her heart.
From that day we were warned not to do this.
Baarh is a small red fruit. We guard our hearts.

Comprehensive

Tutumantu is like hopscotch. Kwani-kwani is like hide-and-seek.
When my sister came back to Africa she could only speak
English. Sometimes we fought in bed because she didn't know
what I was saying. I like Africa better than England.
My mother says You will like it when we get our own house.
We talk a lot about the things we used to do
in Africa and then we are happy.

Wayne. Fourteen. Games are for kids. I support
the National Front. Paki-bashing and pulling girls'
knickers down. Dad's got his own mini-cab. We watch
the video. *I Spit on Your Grave*. Brilliant.
I don't suppose I'll get a job. It's all them
coming over here to work. Arsenal.

Masjid at six o'clock. School at eight. There was
a friendly shop selling wheat. They ground it at home
to make the evening nan. Families face Mecca.
There was much more room to play than here in London.
We played in an old village. It is empty now.
We got a plane to Heathrow. People wrote to us
that everything was easy here.

It's boring. Get engaged. Probably work in Safeway's
worst luck. I haven't lost it yet because I want
respect. Marlon Frederic's nice but he's a bit dark.
I like Madness. The lead singer's dead good.
My mum is bad with her nerves. She won't
let me do nothing. Michelle. It's just boring.

Ejaz. They put some sausages on my plate.
As I was going to put one in my mouth
a Moslem boy jumped on me and pulled.
The plate dropped on the floor and broke. He asked me in Urdu
if I was a Moslem. I said Yes. You shouldn't be eating this.
It's a pig's meat. So we became friends.

My sister went out with one. There was murder.
I'd like to be mates, but they're different from us.
Some of them wear turbans in class. You can't help
taking the piss. I'm going in the Army.
No choice really. When I get married
I might emigrate. A girl who can cook
with long legs. Australia sounds all right.

Some of my family are named after the Moghul emperors.
Aurangzeb, Jehangir, Batur, Humayun. I was born
thirteen years ago in Jhelum. This is a hard school.
A man came in with a milk crate. The teacher told us
to drink our milk. I didn't understand what she was saying
so I didn't go to get any milk. I have hope and am ambitious.
At first I felt as if I was dreaming, but I wasn't.
Everything I saw was true.

Alphabet for Auden

When the words have gone away
there is nothing left to say.

Unformed thought can never be,
what you feel is what you see,
write it down and set it free
on printed pages, © Me.
I love, you love, so does he –
long live English Poetry.
Four o'clock is time for tea,
I'll be Mother, who'll be me?

Murmur, underneath your breath,
incantations to the deaf.

Here we go again. Goody.
Art can't alter History.

Praise the language, treasure each
well-earned phrase your labours reach.

In hotels you sit and sigh,
crafting lines where others cry,

puzzled why it doesn't pay
shoving couplets round all day.
There is vodka on a tray.
Up your nose the hairs are grey.

When the words done gone it's hell
having nothing left to tell.

Pummel, punch, fondle, knead them
back again to life. Read them

when you doubt yourself and when
you doubt their function, read again.

Verse can say *I told you so*
but cannot sway the status quo

one inch. Now you get lonely,
Baby want love and love only.

In the mirror you see you.
Love you always, darling. True.

When the words have wandered far,
poets patronise the bar,

understanding less and less.
Truth is anybody's guess

and Time's a clock, five of three,
mix another G and T.

Set 'em up, Joe, make that two.
Wallace Stevens thought in blue.

Words drown in a drunken sea,
dumb, they clutch at memory.

Pissed you have a double view,
something else to trouble you.

Inspiration clears the decks –
if all else fails, write of sex.

Every other word's a lie,
ain't no rainbow in the sky.

Some get lucky, die in bed,
one word stubbed in the ashtray. *Dead*.

Head of English

Today we have a poet in the class.
A real live poet with a published book.
Notice the inkstained fingers, girls. Perhaps
we're going to witness verse hot from the press.
Who knows. Please show your appreciation
by clapping. Not too loud. Now

sit up straight and listen. Remember
the lesson on assonance, for not all poems,
sadly, rhyme these days. Still. Never mind.
Whispering's, as always, out of bounds –
but do feel free to raise some questions.
After all, we're paying forty pounds.

Those of you with English Second Language,
see me after break. We're fortunate
to have this person in our midst.
Season of mists and so on and so forth.
I've written quite a bit of poetry myself,
am doing Kipling with the Lower Fourth.

Right. That's enough from me. On with the Muse.
Open a window at the back. We don't
want winds of change about the place.
Take notes, but don't write reams. Just an essay
on the poet's themes. Fine. Off we go.
Convince us that there's something we don't know.

Well. Really. Run along now, girls. I'm sure
that gave an insight to an outside view.
Applause will do. Thank you
very much for coming here today. Lunch
in the hall? Do hang about. Unfortunately,
I have to dash. Tracey will show you out.

Lizzie, Six

What are you doing?
I'm watching the moon.
I'll give you the moon
when I get up there.

Where are you going?
To play in the fields.
I'll give you fields,
bend over that chair.

What are you thinking?
I'm thinking of love.
I'll give you love
when I've climbed this stair.

Where are you hiding?
Deep in the wood.
I'll give you wood
when your bottom's bare.

Why are you crying?
I'm afraid of the dark.
I'll give you the dark
and I do not care.

Education for Leisure

Today I am going to kill something. Anything.
I have had enough of being ignored and today
I am going to play God. It is an ordinary day,
a sort of grey with boredom stirring in the streets.

I squash a fly against the window with my thumb.
We did that at school. Shakespeare. It was in
another language and now the fly is in another language.
I breathe out talent on the glass to write my name.

I am a genius. I could be anything at all, with half
the chance. But today I am going to change the world.
Something's world. The cat avoids me. The cat
knows I am a genius and has hidden itself.

I pour the goldfish down the bog. I pull the chain.
I see that it is good. The budgie is panicking.
Once a fortnight, I walk the two miles into town
for signing on. They don't appreciate my autograph.

There is nothing left to kill. I dial the radio
and tell the man he's talking to a superstar.
He cuts me off. I get our bread knife and go out.
The pavements glitter suddenly. I touch your arm.

I Remember Me

There are not enough faces. Your own gapes back
at you on someone else, but paler, then the moment
when you see the next one and forget yourself.

It must be dreams that make us different, must be
private cells inside a common skull.
One has the other's look and has another memory.

Despair stares out from tube-trains at itself
running on the platform for the closing door. Everyone
you meet is telling wordless barefaced truths.

Sometimes the crowd yields one you put a name to,
snapping fiction into fact. Mostly your lover passes
in the rain and does not know you when you speak.

Words of Absolution

She clings to life by a rosary,
ninety years old. Who made you?
God made me. Pearl died a bairn
and him blacklisted. Listen
to the patterns of your prayers
down the years. What is Purgatory?

The guilt and stain of Original Sin.
Except the Virgin. Never a drink
or tobacco and the legs opened only
for childbirth. Forgive me. With her
they pass the parcel. Don't let the music
stop and me holding it. What do you mean
by the resurrection of the body?

Blessed art thou among women even if
we put you in a home. Only the silent motion
of lips and the fingering of decades.
How do we show that we love God?
Never a slack shilling, but good broth
always on the table. Which are the fasting days?
Mary Wallace, what are the days of abstinence?

Chrism, ash, holy water, beads,
wating for the end of nothing. Granny,
I have committed the Sin of Sodom.
How are we to love one another?
What are the four last things
to be ever remembered? I go to my reward.
Chastity. Piety. Modesty. Longanimity.
How should you finish the day? After
your night prayers what should you do?

Whoever She Was

They see me always as a flickering figure
on a shilling screen. Not real. My hands,
still wet, sprout wooden pegs. I smell the apples
burning as I hang the washing out.
Mummy, say the little voices of the ghosts
of children on the telephone. Mummy.

A row of paper dollies, cleaning wounds
or boiling eggs for soldiers. The chant
of magic words repeatedly. I do not know.
Perhaps tomorrow. If we're very good.
The film is on a loop. Six silly ladies
torn in half by baby fists. When they
think of me, I'm bending over them at night
to kiss. Perfume. Rustle of silk. Sleep tight.

Where does it hurt? A scrap of echo clings
to the bramble bush. My maiden name
sounds wrong. This was the playroom.
I turn it over on a clumsy tongue. Again.
These are the photographs. Making masks
from turnips in the candlelight. In case they come.

Whoever she was, forever their wide eyes watch her
as she shapes a church and steeple in the air.
She cannot be myself and yet I have a box
of dusty presents to confirm that she was here.
You remember the little things. Telling stories
or pretending to be strong. Mummy's never wrong.
You open your dead eyes to look in the mirror
which they are holding to your mouth.

Dear Norman

I have turned the newspaper boy into a diver
for pearls. I can do this. In my night
there is no moon, and if it happens that I speak
of stars it's by mistake. Or if it happens
that I mention these things, it's by design.

His body is brown, breaking through waves. Such white teeth.
Beneath the water he searches for the perfect shell.
He does not know that, as he posts the *Mirror*
through the door, he is equal with dolphins.
I shall name him Pablo, because I can.

Pablo laughs and shakes the seaweed from his hair.
Translucent on his palm, a pearl appears. He is reminded.
Cuerpo de mujer, blancas colinas, muslos blancos.
I find this difficult, and then again easy,
as I watch him push his bike off in the rain.

As I watch him push his bike off in the rain,
I trace his name upon the windowpane.
There is little to communicate, but I have rearranged
the order of the words. Pablo says You want for me
to dive again? I want for you to dive.

Tomorrow I shall deal with the dustman.

Talent

This is the word *tightrope*. Now imagine
a man, inching across it in the space
between our thoughts. He holds our breath.

There is no word *net*.

You want him to fall, don't you?
I guessed as much; he teeters but succeeds.
The word *applause* is written all over him.

$

A one a two a one two three four –
boogie woogie chou chou cha cha chatta
noogie. Woogie wop a loo bop a wop
bim bam. Da doo ron a doo ron oo wop a
sha na? Na na hey hey doo wah did.
Um, didy ay didy shala lala lala lala,
boogie woogie choo choo cha cha bop.
(A woogie wop a loo bam) yeah yeah yeah.

Liverpool Echo

Pat Hodges kissed you once, although quite shy,
in sixty-two. Small crowds in Mathew Street
endure rain for the echo of a beat,
as if nostalgia means you did not die.

Inside phone-booths loveless ladies cry
on Merseyside. Their faces show defeat.
An ancient jukebox blares out *Ain't She Sweet*
in Liverpool, which cannot say goodbye.

Here everybody has an anecdote
of how they met you, were the best of mates.
The seagulls circle round a ferry-boat

out on the river, where it's getting late.
Like litter on the water, people float
outside the Cavern in the rain. And wait.

Back Desk

I am Franz Schubert of Dresden. It was not easy.
Quite soon, I realised my prowess on the violin
was mediocre, but we had to eat.
The piece I wrote ('The Bee', you may remember it)
paid for that winter's clothing, little else.
The children danced in their new clogs
till the strings snapped on the highest note.
I saw him once in Heidelberg, the other Franz.
He was older than I, seemed younger.
Smaller than I, looked taller.

Standing Female Nude

Six hours like this for a few francs.
Belly nipple arse in the window light,
he drains the colour from me. Further to the right,
Madame. And do try to be still.
I shall be represented analytically and hung
in great museums. The bourgeoisie will coo
at such an image of a river whore. They call it Art.

Maybe. He is concerned with volume, space,
I with the next meal. You're getting thin,
Madame, this is not good. My breasts hang
slightly low, the studio is cold. In the tea leaves,
I can see the Queen of England gazing
on my shape. Magnificent, she murmurs,
moving on. It makes me laugh. His name

is Georges. They tell me he's a genius.
There are times he does not concentrate
and stiffens for my warmth.
He possesses me on canvas, as he dips the brush
repeatedly into the paint. Little man,
you've not the money for the arts I sell.
Both poor, we make our living how we can.

I ask him, Why do you do this? Because
I have to. There's no choice. Don't talk.
My smile confuses him. These artists
take themselves too seriously. At night, I fill myself
with wine and dance around the bars. When it's finished,
he shows me proudly, lights a cigarette. I say
Twelve francs, and get my shawl. It does not look like me.

Oppenheim's Cup and Saucer

She asked me to luncheon in fur. Far from
the loud laughter of men, our secret life stirred.

I remember her eyes, the slim rope of her spine.
This is your cup, she whispered, and this mine.

We drank the sweet hot liquid and talked dirty.
As she undressed me, her breasts were a mirror

and there were mirrors in the bed. She said, Place
your legs around my neck, that's right. Yes.

Woman Seated in the Underground, 1941

after the drawing by Henry Moore

I forget. I have looked at the other faces and found
no memory, no love. *Christ, she's a rum one.*
Their laughter fills the tunnel, but it does not
comfort me. There was a bang and then
I was running with the rest through smoke. Thick, grey
smoke has covered thirty years at least.
I know I am pregnant, but I do not know my name.

Now they are singing. *Underneath the lantern
by the barrack gate.* But waiting for whom?
Did I? I have no wedding ring, no handbag, nothing.
I want a fag. I have either lost my ring or I am
a loose woman. No. Someone has loved me. Someone
is looking for me even now. I live somewhere.
I sing the word *darling* and it yields nothing.

Nothing. A child is crying. Mine doesn't show yet.
Baby. My hands mime the memory of knitting.
Purl. Plain. I know how to do these things, yet my mind
has unravelled into thin threads that lead nowhere.
In a moment I shall stand up and scream until
somebody helps me. The skies were filled with sirens, planes,
fire, bombs, and I lost myself in the crowd. Dear God.

War Photographer

In his darkroom he is finally alone
with spools of suffering set out in ordered rows.
The only light is red and softly glows,
as though this were a church and he
a priest preparing to intone a Mass.
Belfast. Beirut. Phnom Penh. All flesh is grass.

He has a job to do. Solutions slop in trays
beneath his hands, which did not tremble then
though seem to now. Rural England. Home again
to ordinary pain which simple weather can dispel,
to fields which don't explode beneath the feet
of running children in a nightmare heat.

Something is happening. A stranger's features
faintly start to twist before his eyes,
a half-formed ghost. He remembers the cries
of this man's wife, how he sought approval
without words to do what someone must
and how the blood stained into foreign dust.

A hundred agonies in black and white
from which his editor will pick out five or six
for Sunday's supplement. The reader's eyeballs prick
with tears between the bath and pre-lunch beers.
From the aeroplane he stares impassively at where
he earns his living and they do not care.

Shooting Stars

After I no longer speak they break our fingers
to salvage my wedding ring. Rebecca Rachel Ruth
Aaron Emmanuel David, stars on all our brows
beneath the gaze of men with guns. Mourn for the daughters,

upright as statues, brave. You would not look at me.
You waited for the bullet. Fell. I say, Remember.
Remember these appalling days which make the world
forever bad. One saw I was alive. Loosened

his belt. My bowels opened in a ragged gape of fear.
Between the gap of corpses I could see a child.
The soldiers laughed. Only a matter of days separate
this from acts of torture now. They shot her in the eye.

How would you prepare to die, on a perfect April evening
with young men gossiping and smoking by the graves?
My bare feet felt the earth and urine trickled
down my legs until I heard the click. Not yet. A trick.

After immense suffering someone takes tea on the lawn.
After the terrible moans a boy washes his uniform.
After the history lesson children run to their toys the world
turns in its sleep the spades shovel soil Sara Ezra . . .

Sister, if seas part us, do you not consider me?
Tell them I sang the ancient psalms at dusk
inside the wire and strong men wept. Turn thee
unto me with mercy, for I am desolate and lost.

The Dolphins

World is what you swim in, or dance, it is simple.
We are in our element but we are not free.
Outside this world you cannot breathe for long.
The other has my shape. The other's movement
forms my thoughts. And also mine. There is a man
and there are hoops. There is a constant flowing guilt.

We have found no truth in these waters,
no explanations tremble on our flesh.
We were blessed and now we are not blessed.
After travelling such space for days we began
to translate. It was the same space. It is
the same space always and above it is the man.

And now we are no longer blessed, for the world
will not deepen to dream in. The other knows
and out of love reflects me for myself.
We see our silver skin flash by like memory
of somewhere else. There is a coloured ball
we have to balance till the man has disappeared.

The moon has disappeared. We circle well-worn grooves
of water on a single note. Music of loss forever
from the other's heart which turns my own to stone.
There is a plastic toy. There is no hope. We sink
to the limits of this pool until the whistle blows.
There is a man and our mind knows we will die here.

A Healthy Meal

The gourmet tastes the secret dreams of cows
tossed lightly in garlic. Behind the green door, swish
of oxtails languish on an earthen dish. Here are
wishbones and pinkies; fingerbowls will absolve guilt.

Capped teeth chatter to a kidney or at the breast
of something which once flew. These hearts knew
no love and on their beds of saffron rice they lie
beyond reproach. What is the claret like? Blood.

On table six, the language of tongues is braised
in Armagnac. The woman chewing suckling pig
must sleep with her husband later. Leg,
saddle and breast bleat against pure white cloth.

Alter *calf* to *veal* in four attempts. This is
the power of words; knife, tripe, lights, charcuterie.
A fat man orders his *rare* and a fine sweat
bastes his face. There are napkins to wipe the evidence

and sauces to gag the groans of abattoirs. The menu
lists the recent dead in French, from which they order
offal, poultry, fish. Meat flops in the jowls. Belch.
Death moves in the bowels. You are what you eat.

And Then What

Then with their hands they would break bread
wave choke phone thump thread

Then with their tired hands slump
at a table holding their head

Then with glad hands hold other hands
or stroke brief flesh in a kind bed

Then with their hands on the shovel
they would bury their dead.

from Selling Manhattan

(1987)

Dies Natalis

When I was cat, my mistress tossed me sweetmeats
from her couch. Even the soldiers were deferential –
she thought me sacred – I saw my sleek ghost
arch in their breastplates and I purred

my one eternal note beneath the shadow of pyramids.
The world then was measured by fine wires
which had their roots in my cat brain, trembled
for knowledge. She stroked my black pelt, singing

her different, frantic notes into my ear.
These were meanings I could not decipher. Later,
my vain, furred tongue erased a bowl of milk,
then I slept and fed on river rats . . .

She would throw pebbles at the soil, searching
with long, gold nails for logic in chaos;
or bathe at night in the moon's pool,
dissolving its light into wobbling pearls.

I was there, my collar of jewels and eyes shining,
my small heart impartial. Even now, at my spine's base,
the memory of a tail stirs idly, defining that night.
Cool breeze. Eucalyptus. Map of stars above

which told us nothing, randomly scattered like pebbles.
The man who feared me came at dawn, fought her
until she moaned into stillness, her ringed hand
with its pattern of death, palm up near my face.

*

Then a breath of sea air after blank decades,
my wings applauding this new shape. Far below,
the waves envied the sky, straining for blueness,
muttering in syllables of fish. I trod air, laughing,

what space was salt was safe. A speck became a ship,
filling its white sails like gulping lungs. Food swam.
I swooped, pincered the world in my beak, then soared
across the sun. The great whales lamented the past,

wet years away, sending their bleak songs back
and forth between themselves. I hovered, listening,
as water slowly quenched fire. My cross on the surface
followed, marking where I was in the middle of nowhere . . .

Six days later found me circling the ship. Men's voices
came over the side in scraps. I warned patiently
in my private language, weighed down with loneliness.
Even the wind had dropped. The sea stood still,

flicked out its sharks, and the timber wheezed.
I could only be bird, as the wheel of the day turned slowly
between sun and moon. When night fell, it was stale,
unbearably quiet, holding the breath of the dead.

The egg was in my gut, nursing its own deaths
in a delicate shell. I remember its round weight
persistently pressing; opening my bowel onto the deck
near a young sailor, the harsh sound my cry made then.

*

But when I loved, I thought that was all I had done.
It was very ordinary, an ordinary place, the river
filthy, and with no sunset to speak of. She spoke
in a local accent, laughing at mine, kissed

with her tongue. This changed me. Christ, sweetheart,
marry me, I'll go mad. A dog barked. She ran off,
teasing, and back down the path came Happen you will . . .
Afterwards, because she asked, I told her my prospects,

branded her white neck. She promised herself
in exchange for a diamond ring. The sluggish water
shrugged past as we did it again. We whispered
false vows which would ruin our lives . . .

I cannot recall more pain. There were things one could buy
to please her, but she kept herself apart, spitefully
guarding the password. My body repelled her. Sweat.
Sinew. All that had to be hunched away in nylon sheets.

We loathed in the same dull air till silver presents came,
our two hands clasping one knife to cut a stale cake. One day,
the letter. Surgery. When the treatment did not work,
she died. I cried over the wishbone body, wondering

what was familiar, watching myself from a long way off.
I carried the remains in an urn to the allotment,
trying to remember the feel of her, but it was years,
years, and what blew back in my face was grey ash, dust.

*

Now hushed voices say I have my mother's look.
Once again, there is light. The same light. I talk
to myself in shapes, though something is constantly changing
the world, rearranging the face which stares at mine.

Most of the time I am hungry, sucking on dry air
till it gives in, turning milky and warm. Sleep
is dreamless, but when I awake I have more
to contemplate. They are trying to label me,

translate me into the right word. My small sounds
bring a bitter finger to my mouth, a taste
which cannot help or comfort me. I recall
and release in a sigh the journey here . . .

The man and woman are different colours and I
am both of them. These strangers own me,
pass me between them chanting my new name. They wrap
and unwrap me, a surprise they want to have again,

mouthing their tickly love to my smooth, dark flesh.
The days are mosaic, telling a story for the years
to come. I suck my thumb. New skin thickens
on my skull, to keep the moments I have lived before

locked in. I will lose my memory, learn words
which barely stretch to cover what remains unsaid. Mantras
of consolation come from those who keep my portrait
in their eyes. And when they disappear, I cry.

Homesick

When we love, when we tell ourselves we do,
we are pining for first love, somewhen,
before we thought of wanting it. When we rearrange
the rooms we end up living in, we are looking
for first light, the arrangement of light,
that time, before we knew to call it light.

Or talk of music, when we say
we cannot talk of it, but play again
C major, A flat minor, we are straining
for first sound, what we heard once,
then, in lost chords, wordless languages.

What country do we come from? This one?
The one where the sun burns
when we have night? The one
the moon chills; elsewhere, possible?

Why is our love imperfect,
music only echo of itself,
the light wrong?

We scratch in dust with sticks,
dying of homesickness
for when, where, what.

The Dummy

Balancing me with your hand up my back, listening
to the voice you gave me croaking for truth, you keep
me at it. Your lips don't move, but your eyes look
desperate as hell. Ask me something difficult.

Maybe we could sing together? Just teach me
the right words, I learn fast. Don't stare like that.
I'll start where you leave off. I can't tell you
anything if you don't throw me a cue line. We're dying

a death right here. Can you dance? No. I don't suppose
you'd be doing this if you could dance. Right? Why do you
keep me in that black box? I can ask questions too,
you know. I can see that worries you. Tough.

So funny things happen to everyone on the way to most places.
Come on. You can do getter than that, can't you?

Model Village

See the cows placed just so on the green hill.
Cows say *Moo*. The sheep look like little clouds,
don't they? Sheep say *Baa*. Grass is green
and the pillar box is red. Wouldn't it be strange
if grass were red? This is the graveyard
where the villagers bury their dead. Miss Maiden
lives opposite in her cottage. She has a cat.
The cat says *Miaow*. What does Miss Maiden say?

I poisoned her, but no one knows. Mother, I said,
drink your tea. Arsenic. Four sugars. He waited
years for me, but she had more patience. One day,
he didn't come back. I looked in the mirror,
saw her grey hair, her lips of reproach. I found
the idea in a paperback. I loved him, you see,
who never so much as laid a finger. Perhaps now
you've learnt your lesson, she said, pouring
another cup. Yes, Mother, yes. Drink it all up.

The white fence around the farmyard
looks as though it's smiling, The hens are tidying
the yard. Hens say *Cluck* and give us eggs. Pigs
are pink and give us sausages. *Oink*, they say.
Wouldn't it be strange if hens laid sausages?
Hee-haw says the donkey. The farmhouse
is yellow and shines brightly in the sun. Notice
the horse. Horses say *Neigh*. What does the Farmer say?

To tell the truth, it haunts me. I'm a simple man,
not given to fancy. The flock was ahead of me,
the dog doing his job like a good 'un. Then

I saw it. Even the animals stiffened in fright. Look,
I understand the earth, treat death and birth
the same. A fistful of soil tells me plainly
what I need to know. You plant, you grow, you reap.
But since then, sleep has been difficult. When I shovel
deep down, I'm searching for something. Digging, desperately.

There's the church and there's the steeple.
Open the door and there are the people. Pigeons
roost in the church roof. Pigeons say *Coo*.
The church bells say *Ding-dong*, calling
the faithful to worship. What God says
can be read in the Bible. See the Postman's dog
waiting patiently outside church. *Woof*, he says.
Amen, says the congregation. What does Vicar say?

Now they have all gone, I shall dress up
as a choirboy. I have shaved my legs. How smooth
they look. Smooth, pink knees. If I am not good,
I shall deserve punishment. Perhaps the choirmistress
will catch me smoking behind the organ. A good boy
would own up. I am naughty. I can feel
the naughtiness under my smock. Smooth, pink naughtiness.
The choirmistress shall wear boots and put me
over her lap. I tremble and dissolve into childhood.

Quack, say the ducks on the village pond. Did you
see the frog? Frogs say *Croak*. The village-folk shop
at the butcher's, the baker's, the candlestick maker's.
The Grocer has a parrot. Parrots say *Pretty Polly*
and *Who's a pretty boy then?* The Vicar is nervous
of parrots, isn't he? Miss Maiden is nervous
of Vicar and the Farmer is nervous of everything.
The library clock says *Tick-tock*. What does the Librarian say?

Ssssh. I've seen them come and go over the years,
my ears tuned for every whisper. This place
is a refuge, the volumes breathing calmly
on their still shelves. I glide between them
like a doctor on his rounds, know their cases. Tomes
do no harm, here I'm safe. Outside is chaos,
lives with no sense of plot. Behind each front door
lurks truth, danger. I peddle fiction. Believe
you me, the books in everyone's heads are stranger . . .

The Brink of Shrieks

(for S.B.)

Don't ask me how, but I've fetched up
living with him. You can laugh. It's no joke
from where I'm sitting. Up to the back teeth.

That *walk*. You feel ashamed going out. So-and-so's
method of perambulation, he calls it. My arse.
Thank God for plastic hips. He'll be queuing.

And the *language*. What can you say? Nothing.
Those wee stones make me want to brain him,
so they do. They're only the tip of the iceberg.

Time who stopped? says I. Ash-grey vests,
you try cleaning them. Heartbreaking. Too many nights
lying in yon ditch, counting. God's truth, I *boil*.

See him, he's not uttered a peep in weeks.
And me? I'm on the brink of shrieks.

Recognition

Things get away from one.
I've let myself go, I know.
Children? I've had three
and don't even know them.

I strain to remember a time
when my body felt lighter.
Years. My face is swollen
with regrets. I put powder on,

but it flakes off. I love him,
through habit, but the proof
has evaporated. He gets upset.
I tried to do all the essentials

on one trip. Foolish, yes,
but I was weepy all morning.
Quiche. A blond boy swung me up
in his arms and promised the earth.

You see, this came back to me
as I stood on the scales.
I wept. Shallots. In the window,
creamy ladies held a pose

which left me clogged and old.
The waste. I'd forgotten my purse,
fumbled; the shopgirl gaped at me,
compassionless. Claret. I blushed.

Cheese. Kleenex. *It did happen.*
I lay in my slip on wet grass,
laughing. Years. I had to rush out,
blind in a hot flush, and bumped

into an anxious, dowdy matron
who touched the cold mirror
and stared at me. Stared
and said I'm sorry sorry sorry.

Absolutely

Thank you. Yes please. After you. Don't mind
my asking this, but is politeness strange?
Don't mention it. What do you think yourself?

The politeness of strangers worries me,
like surgical gloves. Irrational, I know.
Nasties in childhood or in the woodshed.

How very interesting. Magritte opened the door
to a journalist, politely bowed him in, then
booted him up the arse right across the room.

And How Are We Today?

The little people in the radio are picking on me
again. It is sunny, but they are going to make it
rain. I do not like their voices, they have voices
like cold tea with skin on. I go O O O.

The flowers are plastic. There is all dust
on the petals. I go Ugh. Real flowers die,
but at least they are a comfort to us all.
I know them by name, listen. Rose. Tulip. Lily.

I live inside someone else's head. He hears me
with his stethoscope, so it is no use
sneaking home at five o'clock to his nice house
because I am in his ear going Breathe Breathe.

I might take my eye out and swallow it
to bring some attention to myself. Winston did.
His name was in the paper. For the time being
I make noises to annoy them and then I go BASTARDS.

Psychopath

I run my metal comb through the D.A. and pose
my reflection between dummies in the window at Burton's.
Lamplight. Jimmy Dean. All over town, ducking and diving,
my shoes scud sparks against the night. She is in the canal.
Let me make myself crystal. With a good-looking girl crackling
in four petticoats, you feel like a king. She rode past me
on a wooden horse, laughing, and the air sang *Johnny,
Remember Me*. I turned the world faster, flash.

I don't talk much. I swing up beside them and do it
with my eyes. Brando. She was clean. I could smell her.
I thought, Here we go, old son. The fairground spun round us
and she blushed like candyfloss. You can woo them
with goldfish and coconuts, whispers in the Tunnel of Love.
When I zip up the leather, I'm in a new skin, I touch it
and love myself, sighing Some little lady's going to get lucky
tonight. My breath wipes me from the looking glass.

We move from place to place. We leave on the last morning
with the scent of local girls on our fingers. They wear
our lovebites on their necks. I know what women want,
a handrail to Venus. She said *Please* and *Thank you*
to the toffee apple, teddy bear. I thought I was on, no error.
She squealed on the dodgems, clinging to my leather sleeve.
I took a swig of whisky from the flask and frenched it
down her throat. *No*, she said, *Don't*, like they always do.

Dirty Alice flicked my dick out when I was twelve.
She jeered. I nicked a quid and took her to the spinney.
I remember the wasps, the sun blazing as I pulled
her knickers down. I touched her and I went hard,

but she grabbed my hand and used that, moaning . . .
She told me her name on the towpath, holding the fish
in a small sack of water. We walked away from the lights.
She'd come too far with me now. She looked back, once.

A town like this would kill me. A gypsy read my palm.
She saw fame. I could be anything with my looks,
my luck, my brains. I bought a guitar and blew a smoke ring
at the moon. Elvis nothing. *I'm not that type*, she said.
Too late. I eased her down by the dull canal
and talked sexy. Useless. She stared at the goldfish, silent. I grabbed
the plastic bag. She cried as it gasped and wriggled
on the grass and here we are. A dog craps by a lamp post.

Mama, straight up, I hope you rot in hell. The old man
sloped off, sharpish. I saw her through the kitchen window.
The sky slammed down on my school cap, chicken licken.
Lady, *Sweetheart*, *Princess*, I say now, but I never stay.
My sandwiches were near her thigh, then the Rent Man
lit her cigarette and I ran, ran . . . She is in the canal.
These streets are quiet, as if the town has held its breath
to watch the Wheel go round above the dreary homes.

No, don't. One thump did it, then I was on her,
giving her everything I had. Jack the Lad, Ladies' Man.
Easier to say Yes. Easier to stay a child, wide-eyed
at the top of the helter-skelter. You get one chance in this life
and if you screw it you're done for, uncle, no mistake.
She lost a tooth. I picked her up, dead slim, and slid her in.
A girl like that should have a paid-up solitaire and high hopes,
but she asked for it. A right-well knackered outragement.

My reflection sucks a sour Woodbine and buys me a drink. Here's
looking at you. Deep down I'm talented. She found out. Don't mess
with me, angel, I'm no nutter. Over in the corner, a dead ringer
for Ruth Ellis smears a farewell kiss on the lip of a gin and lime.
The barman calls Time. Bang in the centre of my skull,
there's a strange coolness. I could almost fly. Tomorrow
will find me elsewhere, with a loss of memory. Drink up son,
the world's your fucking oyster. Awopbopaloobop alopbimbam.

Every Good Boy

I put this breve down, knowing in my head
the sound it makes before I play a note.
C sharp is D flat, changing if I place it here,
or here, or there. Listen. I mostly use a minor key.

These days, the world lacks harmony. The inner cities
riot in my inner ear. *Discord*, say the critics,
but that is what I hear; even in this quiet room
where I deploy blatant consecutive fifths, a hooligan.

That time I was mugged, I came back here
and sat for hours in silence. I have only ever wanted
to compose. The world strikes me and I make
my sound. I make no claim to greatness.

If they were caught, I would like half an hour
together, to show how this phrase, here, excites,
how the smash of broken glass is turned
into a new motif. I would like to share that with them.

Statement

It happened like this. I shall never forget. Da
was drunk again, came in from the yard
with his clenched face like a big fist, leaving
the back door open . . . that low moon, full
and dangerous, at the end of the close. *Jesus Christ,*
he said, *I'd be better dead*, picked up the old clock
from the mantelpiece and flung it on the fire.

It burned till morning came. He kept her up
all night, shouting the bad bits over again
till she put her head in her hands and wept.
Her apron was a map of Ireland. He jabbed
his finger to the North, bruising her breast, yelled
There! There! God's truth, she tried to kiss him,
though Tom's near twenty-one and that was the last time.

Then she starts . . . *In the warfare against the devil,*
the world, and the flesh, on whom must we depend?
and he's ripped the floorboard up. No chance. Her face
was at the window when they got him, watching him
dance for the Queen's men, sweating blood
doing it. I came running down, said, *Mammy,*
Mammy, and she turned with her arms like the crucifix.

Money Talks

I am the authentic language of suffering. My cold, gold eye
does not blink. Mister, you want nice time? No problem.
I say, *Screw You*. I buy and sell the world. I got
Midas touch, turn bread to hard cash. My million tills
sing through the night, my shining mad machines.
I stink and accumulate. Do you fancy me, lady? Really?

See me pass through the eye of a needle! Whoopee,
I cut Time dead with my sleek facelift. I travel
faster than $-sound. Don't give me away; after all, no one
can eat me. Honey, I'm a jealous God, $-stammering
my one commandment on the calculator. *Love me*.
Under your fingernails I smile up with my black grin.

Don't let my oily manner bother you, Sir, I'll get you
a taxi, get you a limousine. I know a place
where it's raining dollar bills. I got any currency
you want, women and gigolos, metal tuxedos. The party
is one long gold-toothed scream. Have a good day. I am
the big bombs, sighing in their thick lead sheaths OK.

Selling Manhattan

All yours, Injun, twenty-four bucks' worth of glass beads,
gaudy cloth. I got myself a bargain. I brandish
firearms and firewater. Praise the Lord.
Now get your red ass out of here.

I wonder if the ground has anything to say.
You have made me drunk, drowned out
the world's slow truth with rapid lies.
But today I hear again and plainly see. Wherever
you have touched the earth, the earth is sore.

I wonder if the spirit of the water has anything
to say. That you will poison it. That you
can no more own the rivers and the grass than own
the air. I sing with true love for the land;
dawn chant, the song of sunset, starlight psalm.

Trust your dreams. No good will come of this.
My heart is on the ground, as when my loved one
fell back in my arms and died. I have learned
the solemn laws of joy and sorrow, in the distance
between morning's frost and firefly's flash at night.

Man who fears death, how many acres do you need
to lengthen your shadow under the endless sky?
Last time, this moment, now, a boy feels his freedom
vanish, like the salmon going mysteriously
out to sea. Loss holds the silence of great stones.

I will live in the ghost of grasshopper and buffalo.

The evening trembles and is sad.
A little shadow runs across the grass
and disappears into the darkening pines.

Politico

Corner of Thistle Street, two slack shillings jangled
in his pocket. Wee Frank. Politico. A word in the right ear
got things moving. *A free beer for they dockers
and the guns will come through in the morning. No bother.*

Bread rolls and Heavy came up the rope to the window
where he and McShane were making a stand. *Someone
sent up a megaphone, for Christ's sake.* Occupation.
Aye. And the soldiers below just biding their time.

Blacklisted. Bar L. *That scunner, Churchill.* The Clyde
where men cheered theirselves out of work as champagne
butted a new ship. Spikes at the back of the toilet seat.
Alls I'm doing is fighting for wur dignity. Away.

*Smoke-filled rooms? Wait till I tell you . . . Listen,
I'm ten years dead and turning in my urn. Socialism?
These days?* There's the tree that never grew. *Och,
a shower of shites.* There's the bird that never flew.

Stealing

The most unusual thing I ever stole? A snowman.
Midnight. He looked magnificent; a tall, white mute
beneath the winter moon. I wanted him, a mate
with a mind as cold as the slice of ice
within my own brain. I started with the head.

Better off dead than giving in, not taking
what you want. He weighed a ton; his torso,
frozen stiff, hugged to my chest, a fierce chill
piercing my gut. Part of the thrill was knowing
that children would cry in the morning. Life's tough.

Sometimes I steal things I don't need. I joyride cars
to nowhere, break into houses just to have a look.
I'm a mucky ghost, leave a mess, maybe pinch a camera.
I watch my gloved hand twisting the doorknob.
A stranger's bedroom. Mirrors. I sigh like this – *Aah*.

It took some time. Reassembled in the yard,
he didn't look the same. I took a run
and booted him. Again. Again. My breath ripped out
in rags. It seems daft now. Then I was standing
alone amongst lumps of snow, sick of the world.

Boredom. Mostly I'm so bored I could eat myself.
One time, I stole a guitar and thought I might
learn to play. I nicked a bust of Shakespeare once,
flogged it, but the snowman was strangest.
You don't understand a word I'm saying, do you?

The Virgin Punishing the Infant

He spoke early. Not the *goo goo goo* of infancy,
but *I am God*. Joseph kept away, carving himself
a silent Pinocchio out in the workshed. He said
he was a simple man and hadn't dreamed of this.

She grew anxious in that second year, would stare
at stars saying, *Gabriel? Gabriel?* Your guess.
The village gossiped in the sun. The child was solitary,
his wide and solemn eyes could fill your head.

After he walked, our normal children crawled. Our wives
were first resentful, then superior. Mary's child
would bring her sorrow . . . better far to have a son
who gurgled nonsense at your breast. *Googoo. Googoo.*

But I am God. We heard him through the window,
heard the smacks which made us peep. What we saw
was commonplace enough. But afterwards, we wondered
why the infant did not cry. And why the Mother did.

Big Sue and *Now, Voyager*

Her face is a perfect miniature on wide, smooth flesh,
a tiny fossil in a slab of stone. Most evenings
Big Sue is Bette Davis. Alone. The curtains drawn.
The TV set an empty head which has the same
recurring dream. Mushrooms taste of kisses. Sherry trifle
is a honeymoon. *Be honest. Who'd love me?*

Paul Henreid. He lights two cigarettes and, gently,
puts one in her mouth. The little flat in Tooting
is a floating ship. Violins. Big Sue drawing deeply
on a chocolate stick. *Now, Voyager depart. Much,
much for thee is yet in store.* Her eyes are wider,
bright. The precious video unspools the sea.

This is where she lives, the wrong side of the glass
in black and white. To press the rewind,
replay, is to know perfection. Certainty. The soundtrack
drowns out daytime echoes. *Size of her. Great cow.*
Love is never distanced into memory, persists
unchanged. Oscar winners looking at the sky.

Why wish for the moon? Outside the window night falls,
slender women rush to meet their dates. Men whistle
on the dark blue streets at shapes they want
or, in the pubs, light cigarettes for two. Big Sue
unwraps a Mars Bar, crying at her favourite scene.
The bit where Bette Davis says, *We have the stars.*

All Days Lost Days

Living
in and out of the past,
inexplicably
so many things have died
in me.

In and out like a tide,
each tear
holds a tiny hologram.
Even this early
I am full of years.

Here are the little gravestones
where memory
stands in the wild grass,
watching the future
arrive in a line of big black cars.

All days
lost days, in and out of themselves
between dreaming
and dreaming again and half-
remembering.

Foreign

Imagine living in a strange, dark city for twenty years.
There are some dismal dwellings on the east side
and one of them is yours. On the landing, you hear
your foreign accent echo down the stairs. You think
in a language of your own and talk in theirs.

Then you are writing home. The voice in your head
recites the letter in a local dialect; behind that
is the sound of your mother singing to you,
all that time ago, and now you do not know
why your eyes are watering and what's the word for this.

You use the public transport. Work. Sleep. Imagine one night
you saw a name for yourself sprayed in red
against a brick wall. A hate name. Red like blood.
It is snowing in the streets, under the neon lights,
as if this place were coming to bits before your eyes.

And in the delicatessen, from time to time, the coins
in your palm will not translate. Inarticulate,
because this is not home, you point at fruit. Imagine
that one of you says, *Me not know what these people mean.
It like they only go to bed and dream.* Imagine that.

Correspondents

When you come on Thursday, bring me a letter. We have
the language of stuffed birds, teacups. We don't have
the language of bodies. My husband will be here.
I shall inquire after your wife, stirring his cup
with a thin spoon and my hand shall not tremble.
Give me the letter as I take your hat. Mention
the cold weather. My skin burns at the sight of you.

We skim the surface, gossip. I baked this cake and you
eat it. Words come from nowhere, drift off
like the smoke from his pipe. Beneath my dress, my breasts
swell for your lips, belly churns to be stilled
by your brown hands. This secret life is Gulliver,
held down by strings of pleasantries. I ache. Later
your language flares in the heat and is gone.

Dearest Beloved, pretend I am with you . . . I read
your dark words and do to myself things
you can only imagine. I hardly know myself.
Your soft, white body in my arms. When we part,
you kiss my hand, bow from the waist, all passion
patiently restrained. *Your servant, Ma'am.* Now you write
wild phrases of love. The words blur as I cry out once.

Next time we meet, in drawing room or garden,
passing our letters cautiously between us, our eyes
fixed carefully on legal love, think of me here
on my marriage bed an hour after you've left.
I have called your name over and over in my head
at the point your fiction brings me to. I have kissed
your sweet name on the paper as I knelt by the fire.

Telegrams

URGENT WHEN WE MEET COMPLETE STRANGERS DEAR STOP
THOUGH I COUNT THE HOURS TILL YOU ARE NEAR STOP
WILL EXPLAIN LATER DATE TILL THEN CANT WAIT STOP C

COMPLETELY FOGGED WHAT DO YOU MEAN BABY? STOP
CANT WE SLOPE OFF TO MY PLACE MAYBE? STOP
NOT POSS ACT NOT MET WITH RAISON DETRE STOP B

FOR GODS SAKE JUST TRUST ME SWEETHEART STOP
NATCH IT HURTS ME TOO WHEN WERE APART STOP
SHIT WILL HIT FAN UNLESS STICK TO PLAN STOP C

SHIT? FAN? TRUST? WHATS GOING ON HONEY? STOP
IF THIS IS A JOKE IT ISNT FUNNY STOP
INSIST ON TRUTH LOVE YOU BUT STRUTH! STOP B

YES I KNOW DARLING I LOVE YOU TOO STOP
TRY TO SEE PREDIC FROM MY POINT OF VIEW STOP
IF YOU DONT PLAY BALL I WONT COME AT ALL STOP C

PLEASE REPLY LAST TELEGRAM STOP
HAVE YOU FORGOTTEN THAT NIGHT IN MATLOCK? C

NO WAS TRYING TO TEACH YOU LESSON PET STOP
ALSO BECAUSE OF THESE AM IN DEBT STOP
TRUST WHEN NEXT MEET WILL PASSIONATELY GREET STOP B

NO NO NO NO GET IT THROUGH YOUR THICK HEAD STOP
IF SEEN WITH YOU AM AS GOOD AS DEAD STOP
THE WIFE WILL GUESS WEVE BEEN HAVING SEX STOP C

SO YOURE MARRIED? HA! I MIGHT HAVE GUESSED STOP
THOUGHT IT ODD YOU WORE STRING VEST STOP
AS SOON AS I MET YOU I WENT OVER THE TOP
NOW DO ME A FAVOUR PLEASE PLEASE STOP STOP B

Telephoning Home

I hear your voice saying *Hello* in that guarded way
you have, as if you fear bad news, imagine you
standing in our dark hall, waiting, as my silver coin
jams in the slot and frantic bleeps repeat themselves
along the line until your end goes slack. The wet platform
stretches away from me towards the South and home.

I try again, dial the nine numbers you wrote once
on a postcard. The stranger waiting outside stares
through the glass that isn't there, a sad portrait
someone abandoned. I close my eyes . . . *Hello?* . . . see myself
later this evening, two hundred miles and two hours nearer
where I want to be. *I love you.* This is me speaking.

Lovesick

I found an apple.
A red and shining apple.
I took its photograph.

I hid the apple in the attic.
I opened the skylight
and the sun said, *Aah!*

At night, I checked that it was safe,
under the giggling stars,
the sly moon. My cool apple.

Whatever you are calling about,
I am not interested.
Go away. You with the big teeth.

Warming Her Pearls

Next to my own skin, her pearls. My mistress
bids me wear them, warm them, until evening
when I'll brush her hair. At six, I place them
round her cool white throat. All day I think of her,

resting in the Yellow Room, contemplating silk
or taffeta, which gown tonight? She fans herself
whilst I work willingly, my slow heat entering
each pearl. Slack on my neck, her rope.

She's beautiful. I dream about her
in my attic bed; picture her dancing
with tall men, puzzled by my faint, persistent scent
beneath her French perfume, her milky stones.

I dust her shoulders with a rabbit's foot,
watch the soft blush seep through her skin
like an indolent sigh. In her looking glass
my red lips part as though I want to speak.

Full moon. Her carriage brings her home. I see
her every movement in my head . . . Undressing,
taking off her jewels, her slim hand reaching
for the case. Slipping naked into bed, the way

she always does . . . And I lie here awake,
knowing the pearls are cooling even now
in the room where my mistress sleeps. All night
I feel their absence and I burn.

Plainsong

Stop. Along this path, in phrases of light,
trees sing their leaves. No Midas touch
has turned the wood to gold, late in the year
when you pass by, suddenly sad, straining
to remember something you're sure you knew.

Listening. The words you have for things die
in your heart, but grasses are plainsong,
patiently chanting the circles you cannot repeat
or understand. This is your homeland,
Lost One, Stranger who speaks with tears.

It is almost impossible to be here and yet
you kneel, no one's child, absolved by late sun
through the branches of a wood, distantly
the evening bell reminding you, *Home, Home,
Home*, and the stone in your palm telling the time.

Miles Away

I want you and you are not here. I pause
in this garden, breathing the colour thought is
before language into still air. Even your name
is a pale ghost and, though I exhale it again
and again, it will not stay with me. Tonight
I make you up, imagine you, your movements clearer
than the words I have you say you said before.

Wherever you are now, inside my head you fix me
with a look, standing here while cool late light
dissolves into the earth. I have got your mouth wrong,
but still it smiles. I hold you closer, miles away,
inventing love, until the calls of nightjars
interrupt and turn what was to come, was certain,
into memory. The stars are filming us for no one.

from The Other Country

(1990)

Originally

We came from our own country in a red room
which fell through the fields, our mother singing
our father's name to the turn of the wheels.
My brothers cried, one of them bawling, *Home,*
Home, as the miles rushed back to the city,
the street, the house, the vacant rooms
where we didn't live any more. I stared
at the eyes of a blind toy, holding its paw.

All childhood is an emigration. Some are slow,
leaving you standing, resigned, up an avenue
where no one you know stays. Others are sudden.
Your accent wrong. Corners, which seem familiar,
leading to unimagined pebble-dashed estates, big boys
eating worms and shouting words you don't understand.
My parents' anxiety stirred like a loose tooth
in my head. *I want our own country,* I said.

But then you forget, or don't recall, or change,
and, seeing your brother swallow a slug, feel only
a skelf of shame. I remember my tongue
shedding its skin like a snake, my voice
in the classroom sounding just like the rest. Do I only think
I lost a river, culture, speech, sense of first space
and the right place? Now, *Where do you come from?*
strangers ask. *Originally?* And I hesitate.

In Mrs Tilscher's Class

You could travel up the Blue Nile
with your finger, tracing the route
while Mrs Tilscher chanted the scenery.
Tana. Ethiopia. Khartoum. Aswan.
That for an hour, then a skittle of milk
and the chalky Pyramids rubbed into dust.
A window opened with a long pole.
The laugh of a bell swung by a running child.

This was better than home. Enthralling books.
The classroom glowed like a sweet shop.
Sugar paper. Coloured shapes. Brady and Hindley
faded, like the faint, uneasy smudge of a mistake.
Mrs Tilscher loved you. Some mornings, you found
she'd left a good gold star by your name.
The scent of a pencil slowly, carefully, shaved.
A xylophone's nonsense heard from another form.

Over the Easter term, the inky tadpoles changed
from commas into exclamation marks. Three frogs
hopped in the playground, freed by a dunce,
followed by a line of kids, jumping and croaking
away from the lunch queue. A rough boy
told you how you were born. You kicked him, but stared
at your parents, appalled, when you got back home.

That feverish July, the air tasted of electricity.
A tangible alarm made you always untidy, hot,
fractious under the heavy, sexy sky. You asked her

how you were born and Mrs Tilscher smiled,
then turned away. Reports were handed out.
You ran through the gates, impatient to be grown,
as the sky split open into a thunderstorm.

Translating the English, 1989

'. . . and much of the poetry, alas, is lost in translation . . .'

Welcome to my country! We have here Edwina Currie
and the *Sun* newspaper. Much excitement.
Also the weather has been most improving
even in February. Daffodils. (Wordsworth. Up North.) If you like
Shakespeare or even Opera we have too the Black Market.
For two hundred quids we are talking *Les Miserables*,
nods being as good as winks. Don't eat the eggs.
Wheel-clamp. Dogs. Vagrants. A tour of our wonderful
capital city is not to be missed. The Fergie,
The Princess Di and the football hooligan, truly you will
like it here, Squire. Also we can be talking crack, smack
and Carling Black Label if we are so inclined. Don't
drink the H_2O. All very proud we now have
a green Prime Minister. What colour yours? Binbags.
You will be knowing of Charles Dickens and Terry Wogan
and Scotland. All this can be arranged for cash no questions.
Ireland not on. Fish and chips and the Official Secrets Act
second to none. Here we go. We are liking
a smashing good time like estate agents and *Neighbours*,
also *Brookside* for we are allowed four Channels.
How many you have? Last night of Proms. Andrew
Lloyd Webber. Jeffrey Archer. Plenty culture you will be agreeing.
Also history and buildings. The Houses of Lords. Docklands.
Many thrills and high interest rates for own good. Muggers.
Much lead in petrol. Filth. Rule Britannia and child abuse.
Electronic tagging, Boss, ten pints and plenty rape. Queen Mum.
Channel Tunnel. You get here fast no problem to my country
my country my country welcome welcome welcome.

Weasel Words

It was explained to Sir Robert Armstrong that 'weasel words' are 'words empty of meaning, like an egg which has had its contents sucked out by a weasel'.

Let me repeat that we Weasels mean no harm.
You may have read that we are vicious hunters,
but this is absolutely not the case. Pure bias
on the part of your Natural History Book. *Hear, hear.*

We are long, slim-bodied carnivores with exceptionally
short legs and we have never denied this.
Furthermore, anyone here today could put a Weasel
down his trouser leg and nothing would happen. *Weasel laughter.*

Which is more than can be said for the Ferrets opposite.
You can trust a Weasel, let me continue, a Weasel
does not break the spinal cord of its victim with one bite.
Weasel cheers. Our brown fur coats turn white in winter.

And as for eggs, here is a whole egg. It looks like an egg.
It is an egg. *Slurp.* An egg. *Slurp.* A whole egg. *Slurp . . . Slurp . . .*

Poet for Our Times

I write the headlines for a Daily Paper.
It's just a knack one's born with all-right-Squire.
You do not have to be an educator,
just bang the words down like they're screaming *Fire!*
CECIL-KEAYS ROW SHOCK TELLS EYETIE WAITER.
ENGLAND FAN CALLS WHINGEING FROG A LIAR.

Cheers. Thing is, you've got to grab attention
with just one phrase as punters rush on by.
I've made mistakes too numerous to mention,
so now we print the buggers inches high.
TOP MP PANTIE ROMP INCREASES TENSION.
RENT BOY ROCK STAR PAID ME WELL TO LIE.

I like to think that I'm a sort of poet
for our times. My shout. Know what I mean?
I've got a special talent and I show it
in punchy haikus featuring the Queen.
DIPLOMAT IN BED WITH SERBO-CROAT.
EASTENDERS' BONKING SHOCK IS WELL-OBSCENE.

Of course, these days there's not the sense of panic
you got a few years back. What with the box
et cet. I wish I'd been around when the *Titanic*
sank. To headline that, mate, would've been the tops.
SEE PAGE 3 TODAY GENTS THEY'RE GIGANTIC.
KINNOCK-BASHER MAGGIE PULLS OUT STOPS.

And, yes, I have a dream – make that a scotch, ta –
that kids will know my headlines off by heart.
IMMIGRANTS FLOOD IN CLAIMS HEATHROW WATCHER.
GREEN PARTY WOMAN IS A NIGHTCLUB TART.
The poems of the decade . . . *Stuff 'em! Gotcha!*
The instant tits and bottom line of art.

Job Creation

(for Ian McMillan)

They have shipped Gulliver up north.
He lies at the edge of the town,
sleeping.
His snores are thunder in the night.

Round here, we reckon they have drugged him
or we dream he is a landscape
which might drag itself up and walk.

Here are ropes, they said.
Tie him down.
We will pay you.
Tie Gulliver down with these ropes.

I slaved all day at his left knee,
until the sun went down
behind it
and clouds gathered on his eyes

and darkness settled on his shoulders
like a job.

Making Money

Turnover. Profit. Readies. Cash. Loot. Dough. Income. Stash.
Dosh. Bread. Finance. Brass. I give my tongue over
to money, the taste of warm rust in a chipped mug
of tap water. Drink some yourself. Consider
an Indian man in Delhi, Salaamat the *niyariwallah*,
who squats by an open drain for hours, sifting shit
for the price of a chapatti. More than that. His hands
in crumbling gloves of crap pray at the drains
for the pearls in slime his grandfather swore he found.

Megabucks. Wages. Interest. Wealth. I sniff and snuffle
for a whiff of pelf; the stench of an abattoir blown
by a stale wind over the fields. Roll up a fiver,
snort. Meet Kim. Kim will give you the works,
her own worst enema, suck you, lick you, squeal
red weals to your whip, be nun, nurse, nanny,
nymph on a credit card. Don't worry.
Kim's only in it for the money. Lucre. Tin. Dibs.

I put my ear to brass lips; a small fire's whisper
close to a forest. Listen. His cellular telephone
rings in the Bull's car. Golden hello. Big deal. Now get this
straight. *Making a living is making a killing these days.*
Jobbers and brokers buzz. He paints out a landscape
by number. The Bull. Seriously rich. Nasty. One of us.

Salary. Boodle. Oof. Blunt. Shekels. Lolly. Gelt. Funds.
I wallow in coin, naked; the scary caress of a fake hand
on my flesh. Get stuck in. Bergama. The boys from the bazaar
hide on the target range, watching the soldiers fire. Between bursts,
they rush for the spent shells, cart them away for scrap.

Here is the catch. Some shells don't explode. Ahmat
runs over grass, lucky for six months, so far. So
bomb collectors die young. But the money's good.

Palmgrease. Smackers. Greenbacks. Wads. I widen my eyes
at a fortune; a set of knives on black cloth, shining,
utterly beautiful. Weep. The economy booms
like cannon, far out at sea on a lone ship. We leave
our places of work, tired, in the shortening hours, in the time
of night our town could be anywhere, and some of us pause
in the square, where a clown makes money swallowing fire.

Ape

There is a male silverback on the calendar.
Behind him the jungle is defocused,
except in one corner, where trees gargle the sun.

After you have numbered the days, you tear off
the page. His eyes hold your eyes
as you crumple a forest in your fist.

The Legend

Some say it was seven tons of meat in a thick black hide
you could build a boat from, stayed close to the river
on the flipside of the sun where the giant forests were.

Had shy, old eyes. You'd need both those hands for one.
Maybe. Walked in placid herds under a jungly, sweating roof
just breathing; a dry electric wind you could hear a mile off.

Huge feet. Some say if it rained you could fish in a footprint,
fruit fell when it passed. It moved, food happened, simple.
You think of a warm, inky cave and you got its mouth all right.

You dream up a yard of sandpaper, damp, you're talking tongue.
Eat? Its own weight in a week. And water. Some say
the sweat steamed from its back in small grey clouds.

But big. Enormous. Spine like the mast on a galleon.
Ears like sails gasping for a wind. You picture
a rope you could hang a man from, you're seeing its tail.

Tusks like banisters. I almost believe myself. Can you
drum up a roar as wide as a continent, a deep hot note
that bellowed out and belonged to the melting air? You got it.

But people have always lied! You know some say it had a trunk
like a soft telescope, that it looked up along it at the sky
and balanced a bright, gone star on the end, and it died.

Descendants

Most of us worked the Lancashire vineyards all year and a few freak
    redheads died.
We were well-nuked. Knackered. The gaffers gave us a bonus
in Burgdy and Claray. Big fucking deal, we thought, we'd been
    robbing them blind
for months. Drink enough of it, you can juggle with snakes, no
    sweat.

Some nights, me and Sarah went down to the ocean with a few flasks
and a groundsheet and we'd have it off three or four times in a night
that barely got dark. For hours, you could hear the dolphins rearing
    up
as if they were after something. Strange bastards. I like dolphins.

Anyway. She's soft, Sarah. She can read. Big green moon and her
    with a book
of *poetry* her Gran had. Nuke me. Nice words, right enough, and I
    love the girl,
but I'd had plenty. *Winter*, I goes, *Spring, Autumn, Summer, don't
    give me
that crap, Sarah*, and I flung the book over the white sand, into the
    waves,

beyond the dolphins. Click-click. Sad. I hate the bastard past, see,
I'd piss on an ancestor as soon as trace one. *What fucking seasons*,
I says to her, *just look at us now*. So we looked. At each other.
At the trembling unsafe sky. And she started, didn't she, to cry.
Tears over her lovely blotchy purple face. It got to me.

We Remember Your Childhood Well

Nobody hurt you. Nobody turned off the light and argued
with somebody else all night. The bad man on the moors
was only a movie you saw. Nobody locked the door.

Your questions were answered fully. No. That didn't occur.
You couldn't sing anyway, cared less. The moment's a blur, a *Film
   Fun*
laughing itself to death in the coal fire. Anyone's guess.

Nobody forced you. You wanted to go that day. Begged. You chose
the dress. Here are the pictures, look at you. Look at us all,
smiling and waving, younger. The whole thing is inside your head.

What you recall are impressions; we have the facts. We called the
   tune.
The secret police of your childhood were older and wiser than you,
   bigger
than you. Call back the sound of their voices. Boom. Boom. Boom.

Nobody sent you away. That was an extra holiday, with people
you seemed to like. They were firm, there was nothing to fear.
There was none but yourself to blame if it ended in tears.

What does it matter now? No, no, nobody left the skidmarks of sin
on your soul and laid you wide open for Hell. You were loved.
Always. We did what was best. We remember your childhood well.

Liar

She made things up; for example, that she was really
a man. After she'd taken off her cotton floral
day frock she was him all right, in her head,
dressed in that heavy herringbone from Oxfam.
He was called Susan actually. The eyes in the mirror
knew that, but she could stare them out.

Of course, a job; of course, a humdrum city flat;
of course, the usual friends. Lover? Sometimes.
She lived like you do, a dozen slack rope ends
in each dream hand, tugging uselessly on memory
or hope. Frayed. She told stories. *I lived
in Moscow once . . . I nearly drowned . . .* Rotten.

Lightning struck me and I'm here to tell . . . Liar.
Hyperbole, falsehood, fiction, fib, were pebbles tossed
at the evening's flat pool; her bright eyes
fixed on the ripples. No one believed her.
Our secret films are private affairs, watched
behind the eyes. She spoke in subtitles. Not on.

From bad to worse. The ambulance whinged all the way
to the park where she played with the stolen child.
You know the rest. The man in the long white wig
who found her sadly confused. The top psychiatrist
who studied her in gaol, then went back home and did
what he does every night to the Princess of Wales.

Boy

I liked being small. When I'm on my own
I'm small. I put my pyjamas on
and hum to myself. I like doing that.

What I don't like is being large, you know,
grown-up. Just like that. Whoosh. Hairy.
I think of myself as a boy. Safe slippers.

The world is terror. Small you can go *As I
lay down my head to sleep, I pray* . . . I remember
my three wishes sucked up a chimney of flame.

I can do it though. There was an older woman
who gave me a bath. She was joking, of course,
but I wasn't. I said *Mummy* to her. Off-guard.

Now it's a question of getting the wording right
for the Lonely Hearts verse. There must be someone
out there who's kind to boys. Even if they grew.

Eley's Bullet

Out walking in the fields, Eley found a bullet
with his name on it. Pheasants *korred*
and whirred at the sound of gunfire.
Eley's dog began to whine. England
was turning brown at the edges. Autumn. Rime
in the air. A cool bullet in his palm.

Eley went home. He put the tiny missile
in a matchbox and put that next to a pistol
in the drawer of his old desk. His dog
sat at his feet by the coal fire as he drank
a large whisky, then another one, but this
was usual. Eley went up the stairs to his bath.

He was in love with a woman in the town. The water
was just right, slid over his skin as he gave out
a long low satisfied moan into the steam.
His telephone began to ring and Eley cursed,
then dripped along the hall. She was in a call-box.
She'd lied all afternoon and tonight she was free.

The woman was married. Eley laughed aloud
with apprehension and delight, the world
expanded as he thought of her, his dog
trembled under his hand. Eley knelt,
he hugged the dog till it barked. Outside, the wind
knew something was on and nudged at the clouds.

They lay in each other's arms, as if what they had done
together had broken the pair of them. The woman
was half-asleep and Eley was telling himself

how he would spend a wish, if he could have only one
for the whole of his life. His fingers counted
the beads of her back as he talked in the dark.

At ten, Eley came into the bedroom with drinks.
She was combing her hair at the mirror. His eyes
seemed to hurt at the sight. She told him sorry,
but this was the last time. She tried to smile.
He stared, then said her words himself, the way
he'd spoken Latin as a boy. Dead language.

By midnight the moon was over the house, full
and lethal, and Eley alone. He went to his desk
with a bottle and started to write. Upstairs,
the dog sniffed at the tepid bed. Eley held
his head in his hands and wanted to cry,
but *Beloved* he wrote and *forever* and *why*.

Some men have no luck. Eley knew he'd as well
send her his ear as mail these stale words,
although he could taste her still. Nearby, a bullet
was there for the right moment and the right man.
He got out his gun, slowly, not even thinking,
and loaded it. Now he would choose. He paused.

He could finish the booze, sleep without dreams
with the morning to face, the loss of her
sore as the sunlight; or open his mouth
for a gun with his name on its bullet to roar
in his brains. Thunder or silence. Eley wished to God
he'd never loved. And then the frightened whimper of a dog.

Following Francis

Watch me. I start with a low whistle, twist it,
pitch it higher and thinner till the kestrel treads air.
There! I have a genius for this, which I offer
to God. Do they say I am crazy, brother?

Yes, they say that. My own wife said it. *Dropping everything*
and following that fool! You want to be covered
in bird shit? You make me sick. I left anyway,
hurried to the woods to meet him. Francis. Francis.
We had nothing. Later, I wept in his arms like a boy;
his hands were a woman's, plucking my tears off, tasting them.

We are animals, he said.

I am more practical. He fumbles with two sticks
hoping for fire; swears, laughs, cups glow-worms
in his palm while I start up a flame. Some nights
we've company, local accents in the dusk. He sees
my jealousy flare beneath dark trees. He knows.
I know he knows. When he looks at me, he thinks

I cannot tame this.

This evening, Francis preaches to the birds. If he is crazy,
what does that make me? I close my eyes. Tell my children
we move north tomorrow, away from here where the world
sings through cool grass, water, air, a saint's voice.
Tell them that what I am doing I do from choice.

He holds a fist to the sky and a hawk swoops down.

Survivor

For some time now, at the curve of my mind,
I have longed to embrace my brother, my sister, myself,
when we were seven years old. It is making me ill.

Also my first love, who was fifteen, Leeds, I know
it is thirty years, but when I remember him now
I can feel his wet, young face in my hands, melting
snow, my empty hands. This is bereavement.

Or I spend the weekend in bed, dozing, lounging
in the past. Why has this happened? I mime
the gone years where I lived. I want them back.

My lover rises and plunges above me, not knowing
I have hidden myself in my heart, where I rock
and weep for what has been stolen, lost. Please.
It is like an earthquake and no one to tell.

M-M-Memory

Scooping spilt, soft, broken oil
with a silver spoon
from a flagstone floor
into a clay bowl –

the dull scrape of the spoon
on the cool stone,
lukewarm drops in the bowl –

m-m-memory.

Kneel there,
words like fossils
trapped in the roof of the mouth,
forgotten, half-forgotten, half-
recalled, the tongue dreaming
it can trace their shape.

Names, ghosts, m-memory.

Through the high window of the hall
clouds obfuscate the sun
and you sit, exhaling grey smoke
into a purpling religious light
trying to remember everything

perfectly
in time and space
where you cannot.
Those unstrung beads of oil
seem precious now, now
that the light has changed.

Père Lachaise

Along the ruined avenues the long gone lie
under the old stones. For ten francs, a map unravels
the crumbling paths which lead to the late great.
A silent town. A vast, perplexing pause.

The living come, murmuring with fresh flowers, their maps
fluttering like white flags in the slight breeze.
April. Beginning of Spring. Lilies for Oscar,
one red rose for Colette. Remembrance. Do not forget.

Turn left for Seurat, Chopin, Proust, and Gertrude Stein
with nothing more to say. Below the breathing trees
a thousand lost talents dream into dust; decay
into largely familiar names for a stranger's bouquet.

Forever dead. Say these words and let their meaning
dizzy you like the scent of innumerable petals
here in Père Lachaise. The sad tourists stand
by the graves, reciting the titles of poems, paintings, songs,

things which have brought them here for the afternoon.
We thread our way through the cemetery, misquoting
or humming quietly and almost comforted.
Two young men embrace near Piaf's tomb.

Dream of a Lost Friend

You were dead, but we met, dreaming,
before you had died. Your name, twice,
then you turned, pale, unwell. *My dear,
my dear, must this be?* A public building
where I've never been, and, on the wall,
an AIDS poster. Your white lips. *Help me.*

We embraced, standing in a long corridor
which harboured a fierce pain neither of us felt yet.
The words you spoke were frenzied prayers
to Chemistry; or you laughed, a child-man's laugh,
innocent, hysterical, out of your skull. *It's only
a dream,* I heard myself saying, *only a bad dream.*

Some of our best friends nurture a virus, an idle,
charmed, purposeful enemy, and it dreams
they are dead already. In cool restaurants,
over the crudités, the healthy imagine a time
when all these careful moments will be dreamed
and dreamed again. *You look well. How do you feel?*

Then, as I slept, you backed away from me, crying
and offering a series of dates for lunch, waving.
I missed your funeral, I said, knowing you couldn't hear
at the end of the corridor, thumbs up, acting.
Where there's life . . . Awake, alive, for months I think of you
almost hopeful in a bad dream where you were long dead.

Who Loves You

I worry about you travelling in those mystical machines.
Every day people fall from the clouds, dead.
Breathe in and out and in and out easy.
Safety, safely, safe home.

Your photograph is in the fridge, smiles when the light comes on.
All the time people are burnt in the public places.
Rest where the cool trees drop to a gentle shade.
Safety, safely, safe home.

The loveless men and homeless boys are out there and angry.
Nightly people end their lives in the short cut.
Walk in the light, steadily hurry towards me.
Safety, safely, safe home. (Who loves you?)
Safety, safely, safe home.

Girlfriends

derived from Verlaine

That hot September night we slept in a single bed,
naked, and on our frail bodies the sweat
cooled and renewed itself. I reached out my arms
and you, hands on my breasts, kissed me. Evening of amber.

Our nightgowns lay on the floor where you fell to your knees
and became ferocious, pressed your head to my stomach,
your mouth to the red gold, the pink shadows; except
I did not see it like this at the time, but arched

my back and squeezed water from the sultry air
with my fists. Also I remember hearing, clearly
but distantly, a siren some streets away – *de*

da de da de da – which mingled with my own
absurd cries, so that I looked up, even then,
to see my fingers counting themselves, dancing.

Words, Wide Night

Somewhere, on the other side of this wide night
and the distance between us, I am thinking of you.
The room is turning slowly away from the moon.

This is pleasurable. Or shall I cross that out and say
it is sad? In one of the tenses I singing
an impossible song of desire that you cannot hear.

La lala la. See? I close my eyes and imagine
the dark hills I would have to cross
to reach you. For I am in love with you and this

is what it is like or what it is like in words.

The *Darling* Letters

Some keep them in shoeboxes away from the light,
sore memories blinking out as the lid lifts,
their own recklessness written all over them. *My own . . .*
Private jokes, no longer comprehended, pull their punchlines,
fall flat in the sad gaps between endearments. *What
are you wearing?*

Don't ever change.
They start with *Darling*; end in recriminations,
absence, sense of loss. Even now, the fist's bud flowers
into trembling, the fingers trace each line and see
the future then. *Always . . .* Nobody burns them,
the *Darling* letters, stiff in their cardboard coffins.

Babykins . . . We all had strange names
which make us blush, as though we'd murdered
someone, under an alias, long ago. *I'll die
without you. Die.* Once in a while, alone,
we take them out to read again; the heart thudding
like a spade on buried bones.

Away from Home

Somewhere someone will always be leaving open
a curtain, as you pass up the dark mild street,
uncertain, on your way to the lodgings.

You put down your case and a blurred longing
sharpens like a headache. A woman carries
a steamy bowl into the room – a red room –

talking to no one, the pleasant and yawning man
who comes in behind her and kisses her palms.
Miles away, you go on, strumming the privet.

*

The train unzips the landscape, sheds fields
and hedges. On the outskirts of a town, the first houses
deal you their bright cards. The Queen of Hearts. A kitchen.

A suburban king counting his money. Jacks.
Behind the back-to-backs, a bruised industrial sky
blackens, and fills with cooking smells, and rains.

Treacherous puddles lead to the Railway Hotel. *No bar
till 7pm*. At the first drink, a haunted jukebox
switches itself on, reminds you, reminds you.

*

Anonymous night. Something wrong. The bedside lamp
absent. Different air. Against the hazarded wall
a door starts faintly to be drawn.

You mime your way ineptly to a switch,
turn to a single room with shower,
an empty flask, a half-drunk glass of wine.

Calm yourself. By dawn you will have slept again
and gone. You have a ticket for the plane. Check it.
The flight number. Your home address. Your name.

*

Urinous broken phone booths lead you
from street to back street, to this last one
which stands at the edge of a demolition site.

Unbelievably, it works. With a sense of luxury
you light a cigarette. There is time yet.
Your fingers press the numbers, almost sensually.

Tomorrow you return. Below the flyover
the sparkling merging motorways glamorise
the night. The telephone is ringing in your house.

November

How they can ruin a day, the funeral cars proceeding
over the edge of the Common, while fat black crows
leer and jeer in gangs. A parliament all right.

Suddenly the hour is less pleasant than it first appeared
to take a walk and post a harmless, optimistic letter.
Face up to it. It is far too hot for November

and far too late for more than the corpse stopped
at a red light near the Post Office, where you pause
wishing you could make some kind of gesture,

like the old woman who crosses herself as the hearse moves on.

River

At the turn of the river the language changes,
a different babble, even a different name
for the same river. Water crosses the border,
translates itself, but words stumble, fall back,
and there, nailed to a tree, is proof. A sign

in new language brash on a tree. A bird,
not seen before, singing on a branch. A woman
on the path by the river, repeating a strange sound
to clue the bird's song and ask for its name, after.
She kneels for a red flower, picks it, later
will press it carefully between the pages of a book.

What would it mean to you if you could be
with her there, dangling your own hands in the water
where blue and silver fish dart away over stone,
stoon, stein, like the meanings of things, vanish?
She feels she is somewhere else, intensely, simpy because
of words; sings loudly in nonsense, smiling, smiling.

If you were really there what would you write on a postcard,
or on the sand, near where the river runs into the sea?

The Way My Mother Speaks

I say her phrases to myself
in my head
or under the shallows of my breath,
restful shapes moving.
The day and ever. The day and ever.

The train this slow evening
goes down England
browsing for the right sky,
too blue swapped for a cool grey.
For miles I have been saying
What like is it
the way I say things when I think.
Nothing is silent. Nothing is not silent.
What like is it.

Only tonight
I am happy and sad
like a child
who stood at the end of summer
and dipped a net
in a green, erotic pond. *The day
and ever. The day and ever.*
I am homesick, free, in love
with the way my mother speaks.

In Your Mind

The other country, is it anticipated or half-remembered?
Its language is muffled by the rain which falls all afternoon
one autumn in England, and in your mind
you put aside your work and head for the airport
with a credit card and a warm coat you will leave
on the plane. The past fades like newsprint in the sun.

You know people there. Their faces are photographs
on the wrong side of your eyes. A beautiful boy
in the bar on the harbour serves you a drink – what? –
asks you if men could possibly land on the moon.
A moon like an orange drawn by a child. No.
Never. You watch it peel itself into the sea.

Sleep. The rasp of carpentry wakes you. On the wall,
a painting lost for thirty years renders the room yours.
Of course. You go to your job, right at the old hotel, left,
then left again. You love this job. Apt sounds
mark the passing of the hours. Seagulls. Bells. A flute
practising scales. You swap a coin for a fish on the way home.

Then suddenly you are lost but not lost, dawdling
on the blue bridge, watching six swans vanish
under your feet. The certainty of place turns on the lights
all over town, turns up the scent on the air. For a moment
you are there, in the other country, knowing its name.
And then a desk. A newspaper. A window. English rain.

from Mean Time

(1993)

The Captain of the 1964
Top of the Form Team

Do Wah Diddy Diddy, Baby Love, Oh Pretty Woman
were in the Top Ten that month, October, and the Beatles
were everywhere else. I can give you the B-side
of the Supremes one. Hang on. *Come See About Me?*
I lived in a kind of fizzing hope. Gargling
with Vimto. The clever smell of my satchel. Convent girls.
I pulled my hair forward with a steel comb that I blew
like Mick, my lips numb as a two-hour snog.

No snags. The Nile rises in April. Blue and White.
The hummingbird's song is made by its wings, which beat
so fast that they blur in flight. I knew the capitals,
the Kings and Queens, the dates. In class, the white sleeve
of my shirt saluted again and again. *Sir! . . . Correct.*
Later, I whooped at the side of my bike, a cowboy,
mounted it running in one jump. I sped down Dyke Hill,
no hands, famous, learning, *dominus domine dominum.*

Dave Dee Dozy . . . Try me. Come on. My mother kept my
    mascot Gonk
on the TV set for a year. And the photograph. I look
so brainy you'd think I'd just had a bath. The blazer.
The badge. The tie. The first chord of *A Hard Day's Night*
loud in my head. I ran to the Spinney in my prize shoes,
up Churchill Way, up Nelson Drive, over pink pavements
that girls chalked on, in a blue evening, and I stamped
the pawprints of badgers and skunks in the mud. My country.

I want it back. The captain. The one with all the answers. *Bzz*.
My name was in red on Lucille Green's jotter. I smiled
as wide as a child who went missing on the way home
from school. The keeny. I say to my stale wife,
Six hits by Dusty Springfield. I say to my boss, *A pint!*
How can we know the dancer from the dance? Nobody.
My thick kids wince. *Name the Prime Minister of Rhodesia.*
My country. *How many florins in a pound?*

Litany

The soundtrack then was a litany – *candlewick*
bedspread three-piece suite display cabinet –
and stiff-haired wives balanced their red smiles,
passing the catalogue. *Pyrex.* A tiny ladder
ran up Mrs Barr's American Tan leg, sly
like a rumour. Language embarrassed them.

The terrible marriages crackled, cellophane
round polyester shirts, and then The Lounge
would seem to bristle with eyes, hard
as the bright stones in engagement rings,
and sharp hands poised over biscuits as a word
was spelled out. An embarrassing word, broken

to bits, which tensed the air like an accident.
This was the code I learnt at my mother's knee, pretending
to read, where no one had cancer, or sex, or debts,
and certainly not leukaemia, which no one could spell.
The year a mass grave of wasps bobbed in a jam jar;
a butterfly stammered itself in my curious hands.

A boy in the playground, I said, *told me*
to fuck off; and a thrilled, malicious pause
salted my tongue like an imminent storm. Then
uproar. *I'm sorry, Mrs Barr, Mrs Hunt, Mrs Emery,*
sorry, Mrs Raine. Yes, I can summon their names.
My mother's mute shame. The taste of soap.

Nostalgia

Those early mercenaries, it made them ill –
leaving the mountains, leaving the high, fine air,
to go down, down. What they got
was money, dull crude coins clenched
in the teeth; strange food, the wrong taste,
stones in the belly; and the wrong sounds,
the wrong smells, the wrong light, every breath –
wrong. They had an ache *here*, Doctor,
they pined, wept, grown men. It was killing them.

It was given a name. Hearing tell of it,
there were those who stayed put, fearful
of a sweet pain in the heart; of how it hurt,
in that heavier air, to hear
the music of home – the sad pipes – summoning,
in the dwindling light of the plains,
a particular place – where maybe you met a girl,
or searched for a yellow ball in long grass,
found it just as your mother called you in.

But the word was out. Some would never
fall in love had they not heard of love.
So the priest stood at the stile with his head
in his hands, crying at the workings of memory
through the colour of leaves, and the schoolteacher
opened a book to the scent of her youth, too late.
It was spring when one returned, with his life
in a sack on his back, to find the same street
with the same sign on the inn, the same bell
chiming the hour on the clock, and everything changed.

Stafford Afternoons

Only there, the afternoons could suddenly pause
and when I looked up from lacing my shoe
a long road held no one, the gardens were empty,
an ice-cream van chimed and dwindled away.

On the motorway bridge, I waved at windscreens,
oddly hurt by the blurred waves back, the speed.
So I let a horse in the noisy field sponge at my palm
and invented, in colour, a vivid lie for us both.

In a cul-de-sac, a strange boy threw a stone.
I crawled through a hedge into long grass
at the edge of a small wood, lonely and thrilled.
The green silence gulped once and swallowed me whole.

I knew it was dangerous. The way the trees
drew sly faces from light and shade, the wood
let out its sticky breath on the back of my neck,
and flowering nettles gathered spit in their throats.

Too late. *Touch*, said the long-haired man
who stood, legs apart, by a silver birch
with a living, purple root in his hand. The sight
made sound rush back; birds, a distant lawnmower,

his hoarse, frightful endearments as I backed away
then ran all the way home; into a game
where children scattered and shrieked
and time fell from the sky like a red ball.

Brothers

Once, I slept in a bed with these four men who share
an older face and can be made to laugh, even now,
at random quotes from the play we were in. *There's no way
in the creation of God's earth*, I say. They grin and nod.

What was possible retreats and shrinks, and in my other eyes
they shrink to an altar boy, a boy practising scales,
a boy playing tennis with a wall, a baby
crying in the night like a new sound flailing for a shape.

Occasionally, when people ask, I enjoy reciting their names.
I don't have photographs, but I like to repeat the names.
My mother chose them. I hear her life in the words,
the breeding words, the word that broke her heart.

Much in common, me, with thieves and businessmen,
fathers and UB40s. We have nothing to say of now,
but time owns us. How tall they have grown. One day
I shall pay for a box and watch them shoulder it.

Before You Were Mine

I'm ten years away from the corner you laugh on
with your pals, Maggie McGeeney and Jean Duff.
The three of you bend from the waist, holding
each other, or your knees, and shriek at the pavement.
Your polka-dot dress blows round your legs. Marilyn.

I'm not here yet. The thought of me doesn't occur
in the ballroom with the thousand eyes, the fizzy, movie tomorrows
the right walk home could bring. I knew you would dance
like that. Before you were mine, your Ma stands at the close
with a hiding for the late one. You reckon it's worth it.

The decade ahead of my loud, possessive yell was the best one, eh?
I remember my hands in those high-heeled red shoes, relics,
and now your ghost clatters toward me over George Square
till I see you, clear as scent, under the tree,
with its lights, and whose small bites on your neck, sweetheart?

Cha cha cha! You'd teach me the steps on the way home from Mass,
stamping stars from the wrong pavement. Even then
I wanted the bold girl winking in Portobello, somewhere
in Scotland, before I was born. That glamorous love lasts
where you sparkle and waltz and laugh before you were mine.

The Good Teachers

You run round the back to be in it again.
No bigger than your thumbs, those virtuous women
size you up from the front row. Soon now
Miss Ross will take you for double History.
You breathe on the glass, making a ghost of her, say
South Sea Bubble Defenestration of Prague.

You love Miss Pirie. So much, you are top
of her class. So much, you need two of you
to stare out from the year, serious, passionate.
'The River's Tale' by Rudyard Kipling by heart.
Her kind intelligent green eye. Her cruel blue one.
You are making a poem up for her in your head.

But not Miss Sheridan. Comment vous appelez.
But not Miss Appleby. Equal to the square
of the other two sides. Never Miss Webb.
Dar es Salaam. Kilimanjaro. Look. The good teachers
swish down the corridor in long, brown skirts,
snobbish and proud and clean and qualified.

And they've got your number. You roll the waistband
of your skirt over and over, all leg, all
dumb insolence, smoke rings. You won't pass.
You could do better. But there's the wall you climb
into dancing, lovebites, marriage, the Cheltenham
and Gloucester, today. The day you'll be sorry one day.

Like Earning a Living

What's an elephant like? I say
to the slack-mouthed girl
who answers back, a trainee ventriloquist,
then smirks at Donna. She dunno.
Nor does the youth with the face.
And what would that say, fingered?
I know. Video. Big Mac. Lager. Lager.
What like's a wart-hog? Come on.

Ambition. Rage. Boredom. Spite. How
do they taste, smell, sound?
Nobody cares. Jason doesn't. Nor does his dad.
He met a poet. Didn't know it. Uungh.
What would that aftershave say
if it could think? What colour's the future?

Somewhere in England, Major-Balls,
the long afternoon empties of air, meaning, energy, point.
Kin-L. There just aren't the words for it.
Darren. Paul. Kelly. Marie. What's it like? Mike?

Like earning a living.
Earning a living like.

The Cliché Kid

I need help, Doc, and bad; I can't forget
the rustle of my father's ballgown as he bent
to say goodnight to me, his kiss, his French scent . . .

Give me a shot of something. Or the sound of Ma
and her pals up late, boozing, dealing the cards.
Big Bertha pissing out from the porch under the stars . . .

It gets worse. Chalk dust. The old schoolroom empty.
This kid so unpopular even my imaginary friend left me
for another child. I'm screwed up, Doc, jumpy . . .

Distraught in autumn, kneeling under the chestnut trees,
seeing childhood in the conkers through my tears.
Bonkers. And me so butch in my boots down the macho bars.

Give me a break. Don't let me pine for that first love,
that faint down on the cheeks, that easy laugh
in my ears, in my lonesome heart, the day that I had to leave.

Sweet Jesus, Doc, I worry I'll miss when a long time dead
the smell the smell the smell of the baby's head,
the fresh-baked grass, dammit, the new-mown bread . . .

Caul

No, I don't remember the thing itself.
I remember the word.
Amnion, inner membrane, *caul*.
I'll never be drowned.

The past is the future waiting for dreams
and will find itself there.
I came in a cloak of cool luck
and smiled at the world.

Where the man asked the woman to tell
how it felt, how it looked,
and a sailor purchased my charm
to bear to the sea.

I imagine it now, a leathery sheath
the length of a palm
empty as mine, under the waves
or spoil on a beach.

I'm all that is left of then. It spools
itself out like a film
a talented friend can recall
using speech alone.

The light of a candle seen in a caul
eased from my crown that day,
when all but this living noun
was taken away.

Away and See

Away and see an ocean suck at a boiled sun
and say to someone things I'd blush even to dream.
Slip off your dress in a high room over the harbour.
Write to me soon.

New fruits sing on the flipside of night in a market
of language, light, a tune from the chapel nearby
stopping you dead, the peach in your palm respiring.
Taste it for me.

Away and see the things that words give a name to, the flight
of syllables, wingspan stretching a noun. Test words
wherever they live; listen and touch, smell, believe.
Spell them with love.

Skedaddle. Somebody chaps at the door at a year's end, hopeful.
Away and see who it is. Let in the new, the vivid,
horror and pity, passion, the stranger holding the future.
Ask him his name.

Nothing's the same as anything else. Away and see
for yourself. Walk. Fly. Take a boat till land reappears,
altered forever, ringing its bells, alive. Go on. G'on. Gon.
Away and see.

Drunk

Suddenly the rain is hilarious.
The moon wobbles in the dusk.

What a laugh. Unseen frogs
belch in the damp grass.

The strange perfumes of darkening trees.
Cheap red wine

and the whole world a mouth.
Give me a double, a kiss.

Small Female Skull

With some surprise, I balance my small female skull in my hands.
What is it like? An ocarina? Blow in its eye.
It cannot cry, holds my breath only as long as I exhale,
mildly alarmed now, into the hole where the nose was,
press my ear to its grin. A vanishing sigh.

For some time, I sit on the lavatory seat with my head
in my hands, appalled. It feels much lighter than I'd thought;
the weight of a deck of cards, a slim volume of verse,
but with something else, as though it could levitate. Disturbing.
So why do I kiss it on the brow, my warm lips to its papery bone,

and take it to the mirror to ask for a gottle of geer?
I rinse it under the tap, watch dust run away, like sand
from a swimming cap, then dry it – firstborn – gently
with a towel. I see the scar where I fell for sheer love
down treacherous stairs, and read that shattering day like braille.

Love, I murmur to my skull, then, louder, other grand words,
shouting the hollow nouns in a white-tiled room.
Downstairs they will think I have lost my mind. No. I only weep
into these two holes here, or I'm grinning back at the joke. This is
a friend of mine. See – I hold her face in trembling, passionate hands.

Moments of Grace

I dream through a wordless, familiar place.
The small boat of the day sails into morning,
past the postman with his modest haul, the full trees
which sound like the sea, leaving my hands free
to remember. Moments of grace. *Like this.*

Shaken by first love and kissing a wall. *Of course.*
The dried ink on the palms then ran suddenly wet,
a glistening blue name in each fist. I sit now
in a kind of sly trance, hoping I will not feel me
breathing too close across time. A face to the name. *Gone.*

The chimes of mothers calling in children
at dusk. *Yes.* It seems we live in those staggering years
only to haunt them; the vanishing scents
and colours of infinite hours like a melting balloon
in earlier hands. The boredom since.

Memory's caged bird won't fly. These days
we are adjectives, nouns. In moments of grace
we were verbs, the secret of poems, talented.
A thin skin lies on the language. We stare
deep in the eyes of strangers, look for the doing words.

Now I smell you peeling an orange in the other room.
Now I take off my watch, let a minute unravel
in my hands, listen and look as I do so,
and mild loss opens my lips like *No.*
Passing, you kiss the back of my neck. A blessing.

The Grammar of Light

Even barely enough light to find a mouth,
and bless both with a meaningless O, teaches,
spells out. The way a curtain opened at night
lets in neon, or moon, or a car's hasty glance,
and paints for a moment someone you love, pierces.

And so many mornings to learn; some
when the day is wrung from damp, grey skies
and rooms come on for breakfast
in the town you are leaving early. The way
a wasteground weeps glass tears at the end of a street.

Some fluent, showing you how the trees
in the square think in birds, telepathise. The way
the waiter balances light in his hands, the coins
in his pocket silver, and a young bell shines
in its white tower ready to tell.

Even a saucer of rain in a garden at evening
speaks to the eye. Like the little fires
from allotments, undressing in veils of mauve smoke
as you walk home under the muted lamps,
perplexed. The way the shy stars go stuttering on.

And at midnight, a candle next to the wine
slurs its soft wax, flatters. Shadows
circle the table. The way all faces blur
to dreams of themselves held in the eyes.
The flare of another match. The way everything dies.

Valentine

Not a red rose or a satin heart.

I give you an onion.
It is a moon wrapped in brown paper.
It promises light
like the careful undressing of love.

Here.
It will blind you with tears
like a lover.
It will make your reflection
a wobbling photo of grief.

I am trying to be truthful.

Not a cute card or a kissogram.

I give you an onion.
Its fierce kiss will stay on your lips,
possessive and faithful
as we are,
for as long as we are.

Take it.
Its platinum loops shrink to a wedding ring,
if you like.
Lethal.
Its scent will cling to your fingers,
cling to your knife.

Steam

Not long ago so far, a lover and I
in a room of steam –

a sly, thirsty, silvery word – lay down,
opposite ends, and vanished.

Quite recently, if one of us sat up,
or stood, or stretched, naked,

a nude pose in soft pencil
behind tissue paper

appeared, rubbed itself out, slow,
with a smoky cloth.

Say a matter of months. This hand reaching
through the steam

to touch the real thing, shockingly there,
not a ghost at all.

Close

Lock the door. In the dark journey of our night,
two childhoods stand in the corner of the bedroom
watching the way we take each other to bits
to stare at our heart. I hear a story
told in sleep in a lost accent. You know the words.

Undress. A suitcase crammed with secrets
bursts in the wardrobe at the foot of the bed.
Dress again. Undress. You have me like a drawing,
erased, coloured in, untitled, signed by your tongue.
The name of a country written in red on my palm,

unreadable. I tell myself where I live now,
but you move in close till I shake, homeless,
further than that. A coin falls from the bedside table,
spinning its heads and tails. How the hell
can I win. How can I lose. Tell me again.

Love won't give in. It makes a hired room tremble
with the pity of bells, a cigarette smoke itself
next to a full glass of wine, time ache
into space, space, wants no more talk. Now
it has me where I want me, now you, you do.

Put out the light. Years stand outside in the street
looking up to an open window, black as our mouth
which utters its tuneless song. The ghosts of ourselves,
behind and before us, throng in a mirror, blind,
laughing and weeping. They know who we are.

Adultery

Wear dark glasses in the rain.
Regard what was unhurt
as though through a bruise.
Guilt. A sick, green tint.

New gloves, money tucked in the palms,
the handshake crackles. Hands
can do many things. Phone.
Open the wine. Wash themselves. Now

you are naked under your clothes all day,
slim with deceit. Only the once
brings you alone to your knees,
miming, more, more, older and sadder,

creative. Suck a lie with a hole in it
on the way home from a lethal, thrilling night
up against a wall, faster. Language
unpeels to a lost cry. You're a bastard.

Do it do it do it. Sweet darkness
in the afternoon; a voice in your ear
telling you how you are wanted,
which way, now. A telltale clock

wiping the hours from its face, your face
on a white sheet, gasping, radiant, yes.
Pay for it in cash, fiction, cab fares back
to the life which crumbles like a wedding cake.

Paranoia for lunch; too much
to drink, as a hand on your thigh
tilts the restaurant. You know all about love,
don't you. Turn on your beautiful eyes

for a stranger who's dynamite in bed, again
and again; a slow replay in the kitchen
where the slicing of innocent onions
scalds you to tears. Then, selfish autobiographical sleep

in a marital bed, the tarnished spoon of your body
stirring betrayal, your heart over-ripe at the core.
You're an expert, darling; your flowers
dumb and explicit on nobody's birthday.

So write the script – illness and debt,
a ring thrown away in a garden
no moon can heal, your own words
commuting to bile in your mouth, terror –

and all for the same thing twice. And all
for the same thing twice. You did it.
What. Didn't you. Fuck. Fuck. That was
the wrong verb. This is only an abstract noun.

Havisham

Beloved sweetheart bastard. Not a day since then
I haven't wished him dead. Prayed for it
so hard I've dark green pebbles for eyes,
ropes on the back of my hands I could strangle with.

Spinster. I stink and remember. Whole days
in bed cawing Nooooo at the wall; the dress
yellowing, trembling if I open the wardrobe;
the slewed mirror, full-length, her, myself, who did this

to me? Puce curses that are sounds not words.
Some nights better, the lost body over me,
my fluent tongue in its mouth in its ear
then down till I suddenly bite awake. Love's

hate behind a white veil; a red balloon bursting
in my face. Bang. I stabbed at a wedding cake.
Give me a male corpse for a long slow honeymoon.
Don't think it's only the heart that b-b-b-breaks.

Stuffed

I put two yellow peepers in an owl.
Wow. I fix the grin of Crocodile.
Spiv. I sew the slither of an eel.

I jerk, kick-start, the back hooves of a mule.
Wild. I hold a red rag to a bull.
Mad. I spread the feathers of a gull.

I screw a tight snarl to a weasel.
Fierce. I stitch the flippers on a seal.
Splayed. I pierce the heartbeat of a quail.

I like her to be naked and to kneel.
Tame. My motionless, my living doll.
Mute. And afterwards I like her not to tell.

Fraud

Firstly, I changed my name
to that of a youth I knew for sure had bought it in 1940, Rotterdam.
Private M.
I was my own poem,
pseudonym,
rule of thumb.
What was my aim?
To change from a bum
to a billionaire. I spoke the English. Mine was a scam
involving pensions, papers, politicians in-and-out of their pram.
And I was to blame.

For what? There's a gnome
in Zurich knows more than people assume.
There's a military man, Jerusalem
way, keeping schtum.
Then there's Him –
for whom
I paid for a butch and femme
to make him come.
And all of the crème
de la crème
considered me scum.

Poverty's dumb.
Take it from me, Sonny Jim,
learn to lie in the mother tongue of the motherfucker you want to
        charm.
They're all the same,
turning their wide blind eyes to crime.
And who gives a damn

when the keys to a second home
are pressed in his palm,
or polaroids of a Night of Shame
with a Boy on the Game
are passed his way at the AGM?

So read my lips. Mo-ney. Po-wer. Fame.
And had I been asked, in my time,
in my puce and prosperous prime,
if I recalled the crumbling slum
of my Daddy's home,
if I was a shit, a sham,
if I'd done immeasurable harm,
I could have replied with a dream:
the water that night was calm
and with my enormous mouth, in bubbles and blood and phlegm,
I gargled my name.

The Biographer

Because you are dead,
I stand at your desk,
my fingers caressing the grooves in the wood
your initials made;
and I manage a quote,
echo one of your lines in the small, blue room
where an early daguerrotype shows you
excitedly staring out
from behind your face,
the thing that made you yourself
still visibly there,
like a hood and a cloak of light.
The first four words that I write are your name.

I'm a passionate man
with a big advance
who's loved your work since he was a boy;
but the night
I slept alone in your bed,
the end of a fire going out in the grate,
I came awake –
certain, had we ever met,
you wouldn't have wanted me,
or needed me,
would barely have noticed me at all.
Guilt and rage
hardened me then,
and later I felt your dislike
chilling the air
as I drifted away.
Your wallpaper green and crimson and gold.

How close can I get
to the sound of your voice
which Emma Elizabeth Hibbert described –
lively, eager and lightly pitched,
with none of the later, bitter edge.
Cockney, a little.

In London Town,
the faces you wrote
leer and gape and plead at my feet.
Once, high on Hungerford Bridge,
a stew and tangle of rags, sniffed by a dog, stood, spoke,
spat at the shadow I cast,
at the meagre shadow I cast in my time.
I heard the faraway bells of St Paul's as I ran.

Maestro. Monster. Mummy's Boy.
My Main Man.
I write you and write you for five hard years.
I have an affair with a thespian girl –
you would have approved –
then I snivel home to my wife.
Her poems and jam.
Her forgiveness.
Her violent love.
And this is a life.
I print it out.
I print it out.
In all of your mirrors, my face;
with its smallish, its quizzical eyes,
its cheekbones, its sexy jaw,
its talentless, dustjacket smile.

The Windows

How do you earn a life going on
behind yellow windows, writing at night
the Latin names of plants for a garden,
opening the front door to a wet dog?

Those you love forgive you, clearly,
with steaming casseroles and red wine.
It's the same film down all the suburban streets,
It's a Wonderful Life. How do you learn it?

What you hear – the doorbell's familiar chime.
What you touch – the clean, warm towels.
What you see what you smell what you taste
all tangible to the stranger passing your gate.

There you are again, in a room where those early hyacinths
surely sweeten the air, and the right words wait
in the dictionaries, on the tip of the tongue you touch
in a kiss, drawing your crimson curtains now

against dark hours. And again, in a kitchen,
the window ajar, sometimes the sound of your radio
or the scent of your food, and a cat in your arms,
a child in your arms, a lover. Such vivid flowers.

Disgrace

But one day we woke to disgrace; our house
a coldness of rooms, each nursing
a thickening cyst of dust and gloom.
We had not been home in our hearts for months.

And how our words changed. Dead flies in a web.
How they stiffened and blackened. Cherished italics
suddenly sour on our tongues, obscenities
spraying themselves on the wall in my head.

Woke to your clothes like a corpse on the floor,
the small deaths of lightbulbs pining all day
in my ears, their echoes audible tears;
nothing we would not do to make it worse

and worse. Into the night with the wrong language,
waving and pointing, the shadows of hands
huge in the bedroom. Dreamed of a naked crawl
from a dead place over the other; both of us. Woke.

Woke to the absence of grace; the still life
of a meal, untouched, wine bottle, empty, ashtray,
full. In our sullen kitchen, the fridge
hardened its cool heart, selfish as art, hummed.

To a bowl of apples rotten to the core. Lame shoes
empty in the hall where our voices asked
for a message after the tone, the telephone
pressing its ear to distant, invisible lips.

And our garden bowing its head, vulnerable flowers
unseen in the dusk as we shouted in silhouette.
Woke to the screaming alarm, the banging door,
the house plants trembling in their brittle soil. Total

disgrace. Up in the dark to stand at the window,
counting the years to arrive here, faithless,
unpenitent. Woke to the meaningless stars, you
and me both, lost. Inconsolable vowels from the next room.

Room

One chair to sit in,
a greasy dusk wrong side of the tracks,
and watch the lodgers' lights come on in the other rooms.

No curtains yet. A cool lightbulb
waiting for a moth. Hard silence.
The roofs of terraced houses stretch from here to how many months.

Room. One second-hand bed
to remind of a death, somewhen. Room.
Then clouds the colour of smokers' lungs. Then what.

In a cold black window, a face
takes off its glasses and stares out again.
Night now; the giftless moon and a cat pissing on a wall. £90pw.

Mean Time

The clocks slid back an hour
and stole light from my life
as I walked through the wrong part of town,
mourning our love.

And, of course, unmendable rain
fell to the bleak streets
where I felt my heart gnaw
at all our mistakes.

If the darkening sky could lift
more than one hour from this day
there are words I would never have said
nor have heard you say.

But we will be dead as we know,
beyond all light.
These are the shortened days
and the endless nights.

Prayer

Some days, although we cannot pray, a prayer
utters itself. So, a woman will lift
her head from the sieve of her hands and stare
at the minims sung by a tree, a sudden gift.

Some nights, although we are faithless, the truth
enters our hearts, that small familiar pain;
then a man will stand stock-still, hearing his youth
in the distant Latin chanting of a train.

Pray for us now. Grade One piano scales
console the lodger looking out across
a Midlands town. Then dusk, and someone calls
a child's name as though they named their loss.

Darkness outside. Inside, the radio's prayer –
Rockall. Malin. Dogger. Finisterre.

Other Poems

A Child's Sleep

I stood at the edge of my child's sleep,
hearing her breathe;
although I could not enter there,
I could not leave.

Her sleep was a small wood,
perfumed with flowers;
dark, peaceful, sacred,
acred in hours.

And she was the spirit that lives
in the heart of such woods;
without time, without history,
wordlessly good.

I spoke her name, a pebble dropped
in the still night,
and saw her stir, both open palms
cupping their soft light;

then went to the window. The greater dark
outside the room
gazed back, maternal, wise,
with its face of moon.

Death of a Teacher

The big trees outside are into their poker game again,
shuffling and dealing, turning, folding, their leaves

drifting down to the lawn, floating away, ace high,
on a breeze. You died yesterday.

When I heard the hour – home time, last bell,
late afternoon – I closed my eyes. English, of course,

three decades back, and me thirteen. You sat on your desk,
swinging your legs, reading a poem by Yeats

to the bored girls, except my heart stumbled and blushed
as it fell in love with the words and I saw the tree

in the scratched old desk under my hands, heard the bird
in the oak outside scribble itself on the air. We were truly there,

present, Miss, or later the smoke from your black cigarette
braided itself with lines from Keats. Teaching

is endless love; the poems by heart, spells, the lists
lovely on the learning tongue, the lessons, just as you said,

for life. Under the gambling trees, the gold light thins and burns,
the edge of a page of a book, precious, waiting to be turned.

Honeymoon

This is true what I say   I saw it
before I died   Pennies first
with the fat black smudged old face of the Queen
then fat slug worms   over and in my eyes.

Felt it before they cried   the dead meat
of my heart   the falling snow
of brain cells far away   stagnant canals
the small dry rattly dice of my last breath.

Knew it deep inside   after an hour of death
inhuman unending cold   after a night
the meaningless sigh of gas   after a week
the stammer of soil on wood   then dark

dark for my honeymoon down in the ground
death's bony bride   my flowers   my creamy shroud.

Munich

6 February 1958

A blizzard of snow like a frenzied crowd.
Nobody cheered or booed.

Two runs at take-off, a free kick stopped by the Ref.
Each held his breath.

Then off the plane, the trudge for an early bath.
A game of cards in the airport, then back.

The engine's shriek, a full-time blow on the whistle.
A manager's scream of wind at the window.

Not over the moon.
A list of names pinned up like a hand-picked team.

To Boil Bacon

First soak the meat
according to its saltiness
in tepid water,

while in the tree outside
a blackbird shakes the weather from its wings.

Cut off from the underside
the brown, then scrape,
then score, the rind,

while on your wet red hand
the hard gold glinting of your ring.

Pierce an onion with a clove,
then put into a saucepan
with the ham, then bring to boil,

while tears jerk in your eyes
to soothe the sting.

Remove all scum.
Replace the lid, then simmer gently,
twenty minutes for each pound,

while children running by outside
whistle and sing.

Allow to cool. Cut off the rind,
then cover with bread raspings,
let it stand,

while on the wireless
the sudden abdication of a king.

Far Be It

Far, far, far
be it from me
this war;

far be it from me
to sieve the news
for poetry.

But the boy who bled
from his stumps of arms
and wasn't dead

held the shape of the crucifix
they hung round my neck
when I was a kid.

Brought to my knees, I genuflect,
shaking with rage and shame
at the TV set.

Backstage

All words by heart as I stand in the dark,
I blank them and breathe, breathe,
they will not leave me.
I am my father's good daughter.
I am my lord's true lover.
I am my own twin brother.
All moves off pat as I wait behind curtains.

All scenes rehearsed as I pause here, certain,
bend at the neck, waist, knees, listen out
for my cue line, inhale, exhale.
I will lose my reason.
I will swallow the poison.
All lines on the tip of my tongue in this dusty gloom.

All text committed as I walked from the green room.
A dead man wrote it.
I have the living throat for a poem.
I have the seeing eyes for a dream.
All dialogue learned as I bide in the wings.

All speeches sure, all lyrics to sing
pitched and prepared, all business timed.
I am the reason and rhyme.
All verbals sorted as I near the stage.

All ad libs inked on the prompter's page.
I will not corpse.
All black as I prowl at the edge of the limelight.

All rewrites scanned as I squint at the spotlight.
I am Queen of Egypt.

All hushed backstage as I pray the script.

Kipling

The base of the heap was the profit made
on the sale of his house,
the mortgage paid and the balance saved
in well-thumbed dosh. On top of that
went the wad dished out by the dude in the hotel bar
who purchased the car, plus the loot from the little guy
who fancied the wife's Diane. The kids' four bikes
went in a weekend job-lot sale
to a priest from Wales, no questions asked,
hard cash, and the caravan to a melancholy man
with a van and a female twin and a tin
of fifty-pound notes. The heap grew,
but he knew what he knew, had a tip
on a cert that would hit paydirt
and he needed more. The art on the walls
made seven grand and the timeshare pad in Portugal
raised seven again. The dog was a bitch,
never been snipped, a pedigree who was ripe
for pups, so that pushed her price up.
He flogged the pension plan to a middleman
from Milton Keynes, plus the unit trusts,
and tossed the stinking tax-free stuff
on the heap. A pawnbroker gave a not-bad price
for his watch, pen, lighter, cufflinks, ID chain, and the wife's
engagement ring fetched as much again on its tod.
A car-boot sale from the back of a cab
took care of his clothes, five suits, three pairs
of boots, a dozen shirts, fifteen jazzy ties.
The children's toys walked at a fiver each
from a cardboard box and the videos vanished
hand over fist to the first in line with a 50p piece.

Ditto, at double the cost and a snip at the price,
over a hundred LPs. Beatles. Beach Boys. Byrds. He peddled
the dodgy plants from the potting shed,
dried in polythene bags, to the local youth
and shifted enough to score a sniff of the harder stuff
for himself. The heap was massive, huge,
so he hawked his arse six times round the park
to top it off, icing the cake, then hired a skip to lug it round
to the betting shop and had it counted, twice,
while he wrote his betting slip out with a sawn-off pen.
Kipling to win. Uttoxeter. Three-ten. After the off, horse riderless
and jockey tossed, he never breathed a word about his loss.

Named For

He was named for his father's father's dog,
a greyhound champ who took on the best
and won, a four-legged friend, fast 'un, hound
with enough bound to reach the first bend
at the bang of the starter's gun, numero uno,
number one. His second name came
from his mother's mother's twin, in the sepia photo
a man with a pencil-thin moustache
and a uniform, who was blown to bits
in a trench in France in World War One. He was named
for his uncle's cousin's fondness for opera, for his
auntie's godmother's love of the work of the bard. Name six
honoured the monarch, seven the PM's spouse, eight
was after his dad's best mate, a bachelor
with a pile in the bank and a terminal cough, nine
was a ponderous name that had been in the family
for years and ten was one that, uttered, could move
his mother to tears, he never knew why. Eleven and twelve
were the next-door neighbours' names and thirteen
to twenty-three were the monikers of the winning team
at Wembley the year he was born. Twenty-four
remembered a saint, a martyr came in at twenty-five
and a priest, a prince, a painter, a pin-up, a pop-star
took him to thirty names. Thirty-one was the name
of the place where his parents met, thirty-two
where they honeymooned and thirty-three the name
of a ship that sank with all hands lost, except for
a second cousin who clung in the retching, heaving sea
to a log. All told, at the end of the day, the first thing
that came to mind when you looked at him was the dog.

Twinned

I have been wined and dined
in the town with which this one is twinned.
The people were kind, I found.

I have walked hand in hand,
scraped two names and a heart with a stick on the sand
in the town with which this one is twinned,
become over-soon over-fond.

And stayed in my room when it rained,
hearing the wind,
with love love love on my mind,
in the town with which this one is twinned,
and pined.

So one day I left it behind –
what little I owned,
whatever I'd gained;
and composed a letter to send,
in the town with which this one is twinned,
to a practical friend.

Then went to see what I'd find
in a different land
where the life, so they said, was grand;
for I had nothing particular planned,
had only the future once read from the palm of my hand
in the town with which this one is twinned,
and a broken heart for somebody somewhere to mend.

To the Unknown Lover

Horrifying, the very thought of you,
whoever you are,
future knife to my scar,
stay where you are.

Be handsome, beautiful, drop-dead
gorgeous, keep away.
Read my lips.
No way. OK?

This old heart of mine's
an empty purse.
These ears are closed.
Don't phone, want dinner,

make things worse.
Your little quirks?
Your wee endearing ways?
What makes you you, all that?

Stuff it, mount it, hang it
on the wall, sell tickets,
I won't come. Get back. Get lost.
Get real. Get a life. Keep schtum.

And just, you must, remember this –
there'll be no kiss, no clinch,
no smoochy dance, no true romance.
You are *Anonymous*. You're *Who*?

Here's not looking, kid, at you.

from The World's Wife

(1999)

Little Red-cap

At childhood's end, the houses petered out
into playing fields, the factory, allotments
kept, like mistresses, by kneeling married men,
the silent railway line, the hermit's caravan,
till you came at last to the edge of the woods.
It was there that I first clapped eyes on the wolf.

He stood in a clearing, reading his verse out loud
in his wolfy drawl, a paperback in his hairy paw,
red wine staining his bearded jaw. What big ears
he had! What big eyes he had! What teeth!
In the interval, I made quite sure he spotted me,
sweet sixteen, never been, babe, waif, and bought me a drink,

my first. You might ask why. Here's why. Poetry.
The wolf, I knew, would lead me deep into the woods,
away from home, to a dark tangled thorny place
lit by the eyes of owls. I crawled in his wake,
my stockings ripped to shreds, scraps of red from my blazer
snagged on twig and branch, murder clues. I lost both shoes

but got there, wolf's lair, better beware. Lesson one that night,
breath of the wolf in my ear, was the love poem.
I clung till dawn to his thrashing fur, for
what little girl doesn't dearly love a wolf?
Then I slid from between his heavy matted paws
and went in search of a living bird – white dove –

which flew, straight, from my hands to his open mouth.
One bite, dead. How nice, breakfast in bed, he said,
licking his chops. As soon as he slept, I crept to the back

of the lair, where a whole wall was crimson, gold, aglow with books.
Words, words were truly alive on the tongue, in the head,
warm, beating, frantic, winged; music and blood.

But then I was young – and it took ten years
in the woods to tell that a mushrooom
stoppers the mouth of a buried corpse, that birds
are the uttered thought of trees, that a greying wolf
howls the same old song at the moon, year in, year out,
season after season, same rhyme, same reason. I took an axe

to a willow to see how it wept. I took an axe to a salmon
to see how it leapt. I took an axe to the wolf
as he slept, one chop, scrotum to throat, and saw
the glistening, virgin white of my grandmother's bones.
I filled his old belly with stones. I stitched him up.
Out of the forest I come with my flowers, singing, all alone.

Queen Herod

Ice in the trees.
Three Queens at the Palace gates,
dressed in furs, accented;
their several sweating, panting beasts,
laden for a long hard trek,
following the guide and boy to the stables;
courteous, confident; oh, and with gifts
for the King and Queen of here – Herod, me –
in exchange for sunken baths, curtained beds,
fruit, the best of meat and wine,
dancers, music, talk –
as it turned out to be,
with everyone fast asleep, save me,
those vivid three –
till bitter dawn.

They were wise. Older than I.
They knew what they knew.
Once drunken Herod's head went back,
they asked to see her,
fast asleep in her crib,
my little child.
Silver and gold,
the loose change of herself,
glowed in the soft bowl of her face.
Grace, said the tallest Queen.
Strength, said the Queen with the hennaed hands.
The black Queen
made a tiny starfish of my daughter's fist,
said *Happiness*; then stared at me,
Queen to Queen, with insolent lust.

Watch, they said, *for a star in the East –*
a new star
pierced through the night like a nail.
It means he's here, alive, newborn.
Who? *Him. The Husband. Hero. Hunk.*
The Boy Next Door. The Paramour. The Je t'adore.
The Marrying Kind. Adulterer. Bigamist.
The Wolf. The Rip. The Rake. The Rat.
The Heartbreaker. The Ladykiller. Mr Right.

My baby stirred,
suckled the empty air for milk,
till I knelt
and the black Queen scooped out my breast,
the left, guiding it down
to the infant's mouth.
No man, I swore,
will make her shed one tear.
A peacock screamed outside.

Afterwards, it seemed like a dream.
The pungent camels
kneeling in the snow,
the guide's rough shout
as he clapped his leather gloves,
hawked, spat, snatched
the smoky jug of mead
from the chittering maid –
she was twelve, thirteen.
I watched each turbaned Queen
rise like a god on the back of her beast.
And splayed that night
below Herod's fusty bulk,
I saw the fierce eyes of the black Queen

flash again, felt her urgent warnings scald
my ear. *Watch for a star, a star.*
It means he's here . . .

Some swaggering lad to break her heart,
some wincing Prince to take her name away
and give a ring, a nothing, nought in gold.
I sent for the Chief of Staff,
a mountain man
with a red scar, like a tick
to the mean stare of his eye.
Take men and horses,
knives, swords, cutlasses.
Ride East from here
and kill each mother's son.
Do it. Spare not one.

The midnight hour. The chattering stars
shivered in a nervous sky.
Orion to the South
who knew the score, who'd seen,
not seen, then seen it all before;
the yapping Dog Star at his heels.
High up in the West
a studded, diamond W.
And then, as prophesied,
blatant, brazen, buoyant in the East –
and blue –
The Boyfriend's Star.

We do our best,
we Queens, we mothers,
mothers of Queens.

We wade through blood
for our sleeping girls.
We have daggers for eyes.

Behind our lullabies,
the hooves of terrible horses
thunder and drum.

Mrs Midas

It was late September. I'd just poured a glass of wine, begun
to unwind, while the vegetables cooked. The kitchen
filled with the smell of itself, relaxed, its steamy breath
gently blanching the windows. So I opened one,
then with my fingers wiped the other's glass like a brow.
He was standing under the pear tree snapping a twig.

Now the garden was long and the visibility poor, the way
the dark of the ground seems to drink the light of the sky,
but that twig in his hand was gold. And then he plucked
a pear from a branch – we grew Fondante d'Automne –
and it sat in his palm like a lightbulb. On.
I thought to myself, Is he putting fairy lights in the tree?

He came into the house. The doorknobs gleamed.
He drew the blinds. You know the mind; I thought of
the Field of the Cloth of Gold and of Miss Macready.
He sat in that chair like a king on a burnished throne.
The look on his face was strange, wild, vain. I said,
What in the name of God is going on? He started to laugh.

I served up the meal. For starters, corn on the cob.
Within seconds he was spitting out the teeth of the rich.
He toyed with his spoon, then mine, then with the knives, the forks.
He asked where was the wine. I poured with a shaking hand,
a fragrant, bone-dry white from Italy, then watched
as he picked up the glass, goblet, golden chalice, drank.

It was then that I started to scream. He sank to his knees.
After we'd both calmed down, I finished the wine
on my own, hearing him out. I made him sit

on the other side of the room and keep his hands to himself.
I locked the cat in the cellar. I moved the phone.
The toilet I didn't mind. I couldn't believe my ears:

how he'd had a wish. Look, we all have wishes; granted.
But who has wishes granted? Him. Do you know about gold?
It feeds no one; aurum, soft, untarnishable; slakes
no thirst. He tried to light a cigarette; I gazed, entranced,
as the blue flame played on its luteous stem. At least,
I said, you'll be able to give up smoking for good.

Separate beds. In fact, I put a chair against my door,
near petrified. He was below, turning the spare room
into the tomb of Tutankhamun. You see, we were passionate then,
in those halcyon days; unwrapping each other, rapidly,
like presents, fast food. But now I feared his honeyed embrace,
the kiss that would turn my lips to a work of art.

And who, when it comes to the crunch, can live
with a heart of gold? That night, I dreamt I bore
his child, its perfect ore limbs, its little tongue
like a precious latch, its amber eyes
holding their pupils like flies. My dream milk
burned in my breasts. I woke to the streaming sun.

So he had to move out. We'd a caravan
in the wilds, in a glade of its own. I drove him up
under cover of dark. He sat in the back.
And then I came home, the woman who married the fool
who wished for gold. At first, I visited, odd times,
parking the car a good way off, then walking.

You knew you were getting close. Golden trout
on the grass. One day, a hare hung from a larch,
a beautiful lemon mistake. And then his footprints,
glistening next to the river's path. He was thin,
delirious; hearing, he said, the music of Pan
from the woods. Listen. That was the last straw.

What gets me now is not the idiocy or greed
but lack of thought for me. Pure selfishness. I sold
the contents of the house and came down here.
I think of him in certain lights, dawn, late afternoon,
and once a bowl of apples stopped me dead. I miss most,
even now, his hands, his warm hands on my skin, his touch.

from Mrs Tiresias

All I know is this:
he went out for his walk a man
and came home female.

Out the back gate with his stick,
the dog;
wearing his gardening kecks,
an open-necked shirt,
and a jacket in Harris tweed I'd patched at the elbows myself.

Whistling.

He liked to hear
the first cuckoo of spring
then write to *The Times*.
I'd usually heard it
days before him
but I never let on.

I'd heard one that morning
while he was asleep;
just as I heard,
at about six p.m.,
a faint sneer of thunder up in the woods
and felt
a sudden heat
at the back of my knees.

He was late getting back.

I was brushing my hair at the mirror
and running a bath
when a face
swam into view
next to my own.

The eyes were the same.
But in the shocking V of the shirt were breasts.
When he uttered my name in his woman's voice I passed out.

*

Life has to go on.

I put it about that he was a twin
and this was his sister
come down to live
while he himself
was working abroad.

And at first I tried to be kind;
blow-drying his hair till he learnt to do it himself,
lending him clothes till he started to shop for his own,
sisterly, holding his soft new shape in my arms all night.

Then he started his period.

One week in bed.
Two doctors in.
Three painkillers four times a day.

And later
a letter
to the powers that be

demanding full-paid menstrual leave twelve weeks per year.
I see him still,
his selfish pale face peering at the moon
through the bathroom window.
The curse, he said, *the curse.*

Don't kiss me in public,
he snapped the next day,
I don't want folk getting the wrong idea.

It got worse.

*

After the split, I would glimpse him
out and about,
entering glitzy restaurants
on the arms of powerful men –
though I knew for sure
there'd be nothing of *that*
going on
if he had his way –
or on TV
telling the women out there
how, as a woman himself,
he knew how we felt.

His flirt's smile.

The one thing he never got right
was the voice.
A cling peach slithering out from its tin.

I gritted my teeth.

And this is my lover, I said,
the one time we met
at a glittering ball
under the lights,
among tinkling glass,
and watched the way he stared
at her violet eyes,
at the blaze of her skin,
at the slow caress of her hand on the back of my neck;
and saw him picture
her bite,
her bite at the fruit of my lips,
and hear
my red wet cry in the night
as she shook his hand
saying, *How do you do*;
and I noticed then his hands, her hands,
the clash of their sparkling rings and their painted nails.

Mrs Aesop

By Christ, he could bore for Purgatory. He was small,
didn't prepossess. So he tried to impress. *Dead men,*
Mrs Aesop, he'd say, *tell no tales.* Well, let me tell you now
that the bird in his hand shat on his sleeve,
never mind the two worth less in the bush. Tedious.

Going out was worst. He'd stand at our gate, look, then leap;
scour the hedgerows for a shy mouse, the fields
for a sly fox, the sky for one particular swallow
that couldn't make a summer. The jackdaw, according to him,
envied the eagle. Donkeys would, on the whole, prefer to be lions.

On one appalling evening stroll, we passed an old hare
snoozing in a ditch – he stopped and made a note –
and then, about a mile further on, a tortoise, somebody's pet,
creeping, slow as marriage, up the road. *Slow*
but certain, Mrs Aesop, wins the race. Asshole.

What race? What sour grapes? What silk purse,
sow's ear, dog in a manger, what big fish? Some days
I could barely keep awake as the story droned on
towards the moral of itself. *Action, Mrs A., speaks louder*
than words. And that's another thing, the sex

was diabolical. I gave him a fable one night
about a little cock that wouldn't crow, a razor-sharp axe
with a heart blacker than the pot that called the kettle.
I'll cut off your tail, all right, I said, *to save my face.*
That shut him up. I laughed last, longest.

Mrs Darwin

7 April 1852

Went to the Zoo.
I said to Him –
Something about that Chimpanzee over there reminds me of you.

Mrs Faust

First things first –
I married Faust.
We met as students,
shacked up, split up,
made up, hitched up,
got a mortgage on a house,
flourished academically,
BA. MA. Ph.D. No kids.
Two towelled bathrobes. Hers. His.

We worked. We saved.
We moved again.
Fast cars. A boat with sails.
A second home in Wales.
The latest toys – computers,
mobile phones. Prospered.
Moved again. Faust's face
was clever, greedy, slightly mad.
I was as bad.

I grew to love the lifestyle,
not the life.
He grew to love the kudos,
not the wife.
He went to whores.
I felt, not jealousy,
but chronic irritation.
I went to yoga, t'ai chi,
feng shui, therapy, colonic irrigation.

And Faust would boast
at dinner parties
of the cost
of doing deals out East.
Then take his lust
to Soho in a cab,
to say the least,
to lay the ghost,
get lost, meet panthers, feast.

He wanted more.
I came home late one winter's evening,
hadn't eaten.
Faust was upstairs in his study,
in a meeting.
I smelled cigar smoke,
hellish, oddly sexy, not allowed.
I heard Faust and the other
laugh aloud.

Next thing, the world,
as Faust said,
spread its legs.
First politics –
Safe seat. MP. Right Hon. KG.
Then banks –
offshore, abroad –
and business –
Vice-chairman. Chairman. Owner. Lord.

Enough? *Encore!*
Faust was Cardinal, Pope,
knew more than God;
flew faster than the speed of sound
around the globe,
lunched;
walked on the moon,
golfed, holed in one;
lit a fat Havana on the sun.

Then backed a hunch –
invested in smart bombs,
in harms,
Faust dealt in arms.
Faust got in deep, got out.
Bought farms,
cloned sheep,
Faust surfed the Internet
for like-minded Bo-Peep.

As for me,
I went my own sweet way,
saw Rome in a day,
spun gold from hay,
had a facelift,
had my breasts enlarged,
my buttocks tightened;
went to China, Thailand, Africa,
returned enlightened.

Turned forty, celibate,
teetotal, vegan,
Buddhist, forty-one.
Went blonde,

redhead, brunette,
went native, ape,
berserk, bananas;
went on the run, alone;
went home.

Faust was in. *A word,* he said,
I spent the night being pleasured
by a virtual Helen of Troy.
Face that launched a thousand ships.
I kissed its lips.
Thing is –
I've made a pact with Mephistopheles,
the Devil's boy.

He's on his way
to take away
what's owed,
reap what I sowed.
For all these years of
gagging for it,
going for it,
rolling in it,
I've sold my soul.

At this, I heard
a serpent's hiss,
tasted evil, knew its smell,
as scaly devil hands
poked up
right through the terracotta Tuscan tiles
at Faust's bare feet
and dragged him, oddly smirking, there and then
straight down to Hell.

Oh, well.
Faust's will
left everything –
the yacht,
the several homes,
the Lear jet, the helipad,
the loot, et cet, et cet,
the lot –
to me.

C'est la vie.
When I got ill,
it hurt like hell.
I bought a kidney
with my credit card,
then I got well.
I keep Faust's secret still –
the clever, cunning, callous bastard
didn't have a soul to sell.

Delilah

Teach me, he said –
we were lying in bed –
how to care.
I nibbled the purse of his ear.
What do you mean?
Tell me more.
He sat up and reached for his beer.

I can rip out the roar
from the throat of a tiger,
or gargle with fire,
or sleep one whole night in the Minotaur's lair,
or flay the bellowing fur
from a bear,
all for a dare.
There's nothing I fear.
Put your hand here –

he guided my fingers over the scar
over his heart,
a four-medal wound from the war –
but I cannot be gentle, or loving, or tender.
I have to be strong.
What is the cure?

He fucked me again
until he was sore,
then we both took a shower.
Then he lay with his head on my lap
for a darkening hour;
his voice, for a change, a soft burr

I could just about hear.
And, yes, I was sure
that he wanted to change,
my warrior.

I was there.

So when I felt him soften and sleep,
when he started, as usual, to snore,
I let him slip and slide and sprawl, handsome and huge,
on the floor.
And before I fetched and sharpened my scissors –
snipping first at the black and biblical air –
I fastened the chain to the door.

That's the how and the why and the where.

Then with deliberate, passionate hands
I cut every lock of his hair.

Anne Hathaway

'Item I gyve unto my wief my second best bed . . .'
(from Shakespeare's will)

The bed we loved in was a spinning world
of forests, castles, torchlight, cliff-tops, seas
where he would dive for pearls. My lover's words
were shooting stars which fell to earth as kisses
on these lips; my body now a softer rhyme
to his, now echo, assonance; his touch
a verb dancing in the centre of a noun.
Some nights I dreamed he'd written me, the bed
a page beneath his writer's hands. Romance
and drama played by touch, by scent, by taste.
In the other bed, the best, our guests dozed on,
dribbling their prose. My living laughing love –
I hold him in the casket of my widow's head
as he held me upon that next best bed.

Queen Kong

I remember peeping in at his skyscraper room
and seeing him fast asleep. My little man.
I'd been in Manhattan a week,
making my plans; staying at two quiet hotels
in the Village, where people were used to strangers
and more or less left you alone. To this day
I'm especially fond of pastrami on rye.

I digress. As you see, this island's a paradise.
He'd arrived, my man, with a documentary team
to make a film. (There's a particular toad
that lays its eggs only here.) I found him alone
in a clearing, scooped him up in my palm,
and held his wriggling, shouting life till he calmed.
For me it was absolutely love at first sight.

I'd been so *lonely*. Long nights in the heat
of my own pelt, rumbling an animal blues.
All right, he was small, but perfectly formed
and *gorgeous*. There were things he could do
for me with the sweet finesse of those hands
that no gorilla could. I swore in my huge heart
to follow him then to the ends of the earth.

For he wouldn't stay here. He was nervous.
I'd go to his camp each night at dusk,
crouch by the delicate tents and wait. His colleagues
always sent him out pretty quick. He'd climb
into my open hand, sit down; and then I'd gently pick
at his shirt and his trews, peel him, put
the tip of my tongue to the grape of his flesh.

Bliss. But when he'd finished his prize-winning film,
he packed his case; hopped up and down
on my heartline, miming the flight back home
to New York. *Big metal bird*. Didn't he know
I could swat his plane from these skies like a gnat?
But I let him go, my man. I watched him fly
into the sun as I thumped at my breast, distraught.

I lasted a month. I slept for a week,
then woke to binge for a fortnight. I didn't wash.
The parrots clacked their migraine chant.
The swinging monkeys whinged. Fevered, I drank
handfuls of river right by the spot where he'd bathed.
I bled when a fat, red moon rolled on the jungle roof.
And after that, I decided to get him back.

So I came to sail up the Hudson one June night,
with the New York skyline a concrete rainforest
of light; and felt, lovesick and vast, the first
glimmer of hope in weeks. I was discreet, prowled
those streets in darkness, pressing my passionate eye
to a thousand windows, each with its modest peep show
of boredom or pain, of drama, consolation, remorse.

I found him, of course. At three a.m. on a Sunday,
dreaming alone in his single bed; over his lovely head
a blown-up photograph of myself. I stared for a long time
till my big brown eyes grew moist; then I padded away
through Central Park, under the stars. He was mine.
Next day, I shopped. Clothes for my man, mainly,
but one or two treats for myself from Bloomingdale's.

I picked him, like a chocolate from the top layer
of a box, one Friday night, out of his room
and let him dangle in the air between my finger
and my thumb in a teasing, lover's way. Then we sat
on the tip of the Empire State Building, saying farewell
to the Brooklyn Bridge, to the winking yellow cabs,
to the helicopters over the river, dragonflies.

Twelve happy years. He slept in my fur, woke early
to massage the heavy lids of my eyes. I liked that.
He liked me to gently blow on him; or scratch,
with care, the length of his back with my nail.
Then I'd ask him to play on the wooden pipes he'd made
in our first year. He'd sit, cross-legged, near my ear
for hours: his plaintive, lost tunes making me cry.

When he died I held him all night, shaking him
like a doll, licking his face, breast, soles of his feet,
his little rod. But then, heartsore as I was, I set to work.
He would be pleased. I wear him now about my neck,
perfect, preserved, with tiny emeralds for eyes. No man
has been loved more. I'm sure that, sometimes, in his silent death,
against my massive, breathing lungs, he hears me roar.

Medusa

A suspicion, a doubt, a jealousy
grew in my mind,
which turned the hairs on my head to filthy snakes,
as though my thoughts
hissed and spat on my scalp.

My bride's breath soured, stank
in the grey bags of my lungs.
I'm foul mouthed now, foul tongued,
yellow fanged.
There are bullet tears in my eyes.
Are you terrified?

Be terrified.
It's you I love,
perfect man, Greek God, my own;
but I know you'll go, betray me, stray
from home.
So better by far for me if you were stone.

I glanced at a buzzing bee,
a dull grey pebble fell
to the ground.
I glanced at a singing bird,
a handful of dusty gravel
spattered down.

I looked at a ginger cat,
a housebrick
shattered a bowl of milk.

I looked at a snuffling pig,
a boulder rolled
in a heap of shit.

I stared in the mirror.
Love gone bad
showed me a Gorgon.
I stared at a dragon.
Fire spewed
from the mouth of a mountain.

And here you come
with a shield for a heart
and a sword for a tongue
and your girls, your girls.
Wasn't I beautiful?
Wasn't I fragrant and young?

Look at me now.

The Devil's Wife

1. Dirt

The Devil was one of the men at work.
Different. Fancied himself. Looked at the girls
in the office as though they were dirt. Didn't flirt.
Didn't speak. Was sarcastic and rude if he did.
I'd stare him out, chewing my gum, insolent, dumb.
I'd lie on my bed at home, on fire for him.

I scowled and pouted and sneered. I gave
as good as I got till he asked me out. In his car
he put two fags in his mouth and lit them both.
He bit my breast. His language was foul. He entered me.
We're the same, he said, That's it. I swooned in my soul.
We drove to the woods and he made me bury a doll.

I went mad for the sex. I won't repeat what we did.
We gave up going to work. It was either the woods
or looking at playgrounds, fairgrounds. Coloured lights
in the rain. I'd walk around on my own. He tailed.
I felt like this: Tongue of stone. Two black slates
for eyes. Thumped wound of a mouth. Nobody's Mam.

2. Medusa

I flew in my chains over the wood where we'd buried
the doll. I know it was me who was there.
I know I carried the spade. I know I was covered in mud.
But I cannot remember how or when or precisely where.

Nobody liked my hair. Nobody liked how I spoke.
He held my heart in his fist and he squeezed it dry.
I gave the cameras my Medusa stare.
I heard the judge summing up. I didn't care.

I was left to rot. I was locked up, double-locked.
I know they chucked the key. It was nowt to me.
I wrote to him every day in our private code.
I thought in twelve, fifteen, we'd be out on the open road.

But life, they said, means life. Dying inside.
The Devil was evil, mad, but I was the Devil's wife
which made me worse. I howled in my cell.
If the Devil was gone then how could this be hell?

3. Bible

I said No not me I didn't I couldn't I wouldn't.
Can't remember no idea not in the room.
Get me a Bible honestly promise you swear.
I never not in a million years it was him.

I said Send me a lawyer a vicar a priest.
Send me a TV crew send me a journalist.
Can't remember not in the room. Send me
a shrink where's my MP send him to me.

I said Not fair not right not on not true
not like that. Didn't see didn't know didn't hear.
Maybe this maybe that not sure not certain maybe.
Can't remember no idea it was him it was him.

Can't remember no idea not in the room.
No idea can't remember not in the room.

4. Night

In the long fifty-year night,
these are the words that crawl out of the wall:
Suffer. Monster. Burn in Hell.

When morning comes,
I will finally tell.

Amen.

5. Appeal

If I'd been stoned to death
If I'd been hung by the neck
If I'd been shaved and strapped to the Chair
If an injection
If my peroxide head on the block
If my outstretched hands for the chop
If my tongue torn out at the root
If from ear to ear my throat
If a bullet a hammer a knife
If life means life means life means life

But what did I do to us all, to myself,
When I was the Devil's wife?

Circe

I'm fond, nereids and nymphs, unlike some, of the pig,
of the tusker, the snout, the boar and the swine.
One way or another, all pigs have been mine –
under my thumb, the bristling, salty skin of their backs,
in my nostrils here, their yobby, porky colognes.
I'm familiar with hogs and runts, their percussion of oinks
and grunts, their squeals. I've stood with a pail of swill
at dusk, at the creaky gate of the sty,
tasting the sweaty, spicy air, the moon
like a lemon popped in the mouth of the sky.
But I want to begin with a recipe from abroad

which uses the cheek – and the tongue in cheek
at that. Lay two pig's cheeks, with the tongue,
in a dish, and strew it well over with salt
and cloves. Remember the skills of the tongue –
to lick, to lap, to loosen, lubricate, to lie
in the soft pouch of the face – and how each pig's face
was uniquely itself, as many handsome as plain,
the cowardly face, the brave, the comical, noble,
sly or wise, the cruel, the kind, but all of them,
nymphs, with those piggy eyes. Season with mace.

Well-cleaned pigs' ears should be blanched, singed, tossed
in a pot, boiled, kept hot, scraped, served, garnished
with thyme. Look at that simmering lug, at that ear,
did it listen, ever, to you, to your prayers and rhymes,
to the chimes of your voice, singing and clear? Mash
the potatoes, nymph, open the beer. Now to the brains,

to the trotters, shoulders, chops, to the sweetmeats slipped
from the slit, bulging, vulnerable bag of the balls.
When the heart of a pig has hardened, dice it small.

Dice it small. I, too, once knelt on this shining shore
watching the tall ships sail from the burning sun
like myths; slipped off my dress to wade,
breast deep, in the sea, waving and calling;
then plunged, then swam on my back, looking up
as three black ships sighed in the shallow waves.
Of course, I was younger then. And hoping for men. Now,
let us baste that sizzling pig on the spit once again.

Mrs Lazarus

I had grieved. I had wept for a night and a day
over my loss, ripped the cloth I was married in
from my breasts, howled, shrieked, clawed
at the burial stones till my hands bled, retched
his name over and over again, dead, dead.

Gone home. Gutted the place. Slept in a single cot,
widow, one empty glove, white femur
in the dust, half. Stuffed dark suits
into black bags, shuffled in a dead man's shoes,
noosed the double knot of a tie round my bare neck,

gaunt nun in the mirror, touching herself. I learnt
the Stations of Bereavement, the icon of my face
in each bleak frame; but all those months
he was going away from me, dwindling
to the shrunk size of a snapshot, going,

going. Till his name was no longer a certain spell
for his face. The last hair on his head
floated out from a book. His scent went from the house.
The will was read. See, he was vanishing
to the small zero held by the gold of my ring.

Then he was gone. Then he was legend, language;
my arm on the arm of the schoolteacher – the shock
of a man's strength under the sleeve of his coat –
along the hedgerows. But I was faithful
for as long as it took. Until he was memory.

So I could stand that evening in the field
in a shawl of fine air, healed, able
to watch the edge of the moon occur to the sky
and a hare thump from a hedge; then notice
the village men running towards me, shouting,

behind them the women and children, barking dogs,
and I knew. I knew by the sly light
on the blacksmith's face, the shrill eyes
of the barmaid, the sudden hands bearing me
into the hot tang of the crowd parting before me.

He lived. I saw the horror on his face.
I heard his mother's crazy song. I breathed
his stench; my bridegroom in his rotting shroud,
moist and dishevelled from the grave's slack chew,
croaking his cuckold name, disinherited, out of his time.

Pygmalion's Bride

Cold, I was, like snow, like ivory.
I thought, *He will not touch me*,
but he did.

He kissed my stone-cool lips.
I lay still
as though I'd died.
He stayed.
He thumbed my marbled eyes.

He spoke –
blunt endearments, what he'd do and how.
His words were terrible.
My ears were sculpture,
stone-deaf, shells.
I heard the sea.
I drowned him out.
I heard him shout.

He brought me presents, polished pebbles,
little bells.
I didn't blink,
was dumb.
He brought me pearls and necklaces and rings.
He called them *girly things*.
He ran his clammy hands along my limbs.
I didn't shrink,
played statue, schtum.

He let his fingers sink into my flesh,
he squeezed, he pressed.
I would not bruise.
He looked for marks,
for purple hearts,
for inky stars, for smudgy clues.
His nails were claws.
I showed no scratch, no scrape, no scar.
He propped me up on pillows,
jawed all night.
My heart was ice, was glass.
His voice was gravel, hoarse.
He talked white black.

So I changed tack,
grew warm, like candle wax,
kissed back,
was soft, was pliable,
began to moan,
got hot, got wild,
arched, coiled, writhed,
begged for his child,
and at the climax
screamed my head off –
all an act.

And haven't seen him since.
Simple as that.

Mrs Rip Van Winkle

I sank like a stone
into the still, deep waters of late middle age,
aching from head to foot.

I took up food
and gave up exercise.
It did me good.

And while he slept
I found some hobbies for myself.
Painting. Seeing the sights I'd always dreamed about:

The Leaning Tower.
The Pyramids. The Taj Mahal.
I made a little watercolour of them all.

But what was best,
what hands-down beat the rest,
was saying a none-too-fond farewell to sex.

Until the day
I came home with this pastel of Niagara
and he was sitting up in bed rattling Viagra.

Frau Freud

Ladies, for argument's sake, let us say
that I've seen my fair share of ding-a-ling, member and jock,
of todger and nudger and percy and cock, of tackle,
of three-for-a-bob, of willy and winky; in fact,
you could say, I'm as au fait with Hunt-the-Salami
as Ms M. Lewinsky – equally sick up to here
with the beef bayonet, the pork sword, the saveloy,
love-muscle, night-crawler, dong, the dick, prick,
dipstick and wick, the rammer, the slammer, the rupert,
the shlong. Don't get me wrong, I've no axe to grind
with the snake in the trousers, the wife's best friend,
the weapon, the python – I suppose what I mean is,
ladies, dear ladies, the average penis – not pretty . . .
the squint of its envious solitary eye . . . one's feeling of pity . . .

Salome

I'd done it before
(and doubtless I'll do it again,
sooner or later)
woke up with a head on the pillow beside me – whose? –
what did it matter?
Good-looking, of course, dark hair, rather matted,
the reddish beard several shades lighter;
with very deep lines round the eyes,
from pain, I'd guess, maybe laughter;
and a beautiful crimson mouth that obviously knew
how to flatter . . .
which I kissed . . .
Colder than pewter.
Strange. What was his name? Peter?

Simon? Andrew? John? I knew I'd feel better
for tea, dry toast, no butter,
so rang for the maid.
And, indeed, her innocent clatter
of cups and plates,
her clearing of clutter,
her regional patter,
were just what I needed –
hungover and wrecked as I was from a night on the batter.

Never again!
I needed to clean up my act,
get fitter,
cut out the booze and the fags and the sex.
Yes. And as for the latter,
it was time to turf out the blighter,

the beater or biter,
who'd come like a lamb to the slaughter
to Salome's bed.

In the mirror, I saw my eyes glitter.
I flung back the sticky red sheets
and there, like I said – and ain't life a bitch –
was his head on a platter.

The Kray Sisters

There go the twins! geezers would say
when we walked down the frog and toad
in our Savile Row whistle and flutes, tailored
to flatter our thr'penny bits, which were big,
like our East End hearts. No one could tell us apart,
except when one twin wore glasses or shades
over two of our four mince pies. Oh, London, London,
London Town, made for a girl and her double
to swagger around, or be driven at speed
in the back of an Austin Princess, black,
up West to a club; to order up bubbly, the best,
in a bucket of ice. Garland singing that night. Nice.

Childhood. When we were God Forbids, we lived
with our grandmother – God Rest Her Soul – a tough suffragette
who'd knocked out a Grand National horse, name of
Ballytown Boy, with one punch, in front of the King,
for the cause. She was known round our manor thereafter
as Cannonball Vi. By the time we were six,
we were sat at her skirts, inhaling the juniper fumes
of her Vera Lynn; hearing the stories of Emmeline's Army
before and after the '14 war. Diamond ladies,
they were, those birds who fought for the Vote, salt
of the earth. And maybe this marked us for ever,
because of the loss of our mother, who died giving birth

to the pair of unusual us. Straight up, we knew,
even then, what we wanted to be; had, you could say,
a vocation. We wanted respect for the way
we entered a bar, or handled a car, or shrivelled

a hard-on with simply a menacing look, a threatening word
in a hairy ear, a knee in the orchestra stalls. Belles
of the balls. Queens of the Smoke. We dreamed it all,
trudging for miles, holding the hand of the past, learning
the map of the city under our feet; clocking the boozers,
back alleys, mews, the churches and bridges, the parks,
the Underground stations, the grand hotels where Vita and Violet,
pin-ups of ours, had given it wallop. We stared from Hungerford
    Bridge
as the lights of London tarted up the old Thames. All right,

we made our mistakes in those early years. We were soft
when we should have been hard; enrolled a few girls
in the firm who were well out of order – two of them
getting engaged; a third sneaking back up the Mile End Road
every night to be some plonker's wife. Rule Number One –
A boyfriend's for Christmas, not just for life.
But we learned – and our twenty-first birthday saw us installed
in the first of our clubs, Ballbreakers, just off
Evering Road. The word got around and about
that any woman in trouble could come to the Krays,
no questions asked, for Protection. We'd soon earned the clout
and the dosh and respect for a move, Piccadilly way,

to a classier gaff – to the club at the heart of our legend,
Prickteasers. We admit, bang to rights, that the fruits
of feminism – fact – made us rich, feared, famous,
friends of the stars. Have a good butcher's at these –
there we are forever in glamorous black and white,
assertively staring out next to Germaine, Bardot,
Twiggy and Lulu, Dusty and Yoko, Bassey, Babs,
Sandy, Diana Dors. And London was safer then
on account of us. Look at the letters we get –

*Dear Twins, them were the good old days when you ruled
the streets. There was none of this mugging old ladies
or touching young girls.* We hear what's being said.

Remember us at our peak, in our prime, dressed to kill
and swaggering into our club, stroke of twelve,
the evening we leaned on Sinatra to sing for free.
There was always a bit of a buzz when we entered, stopping
at favoured tables, giving a nod or a wink, buying someone
a drink, lighting a fag, lending an ear. That particular night
something electric, trembling, blue, crackled the air. Leave us both
    there,
spotlit, strong, at the top of our world, with Sinatra drawling, *And
    here's*
a song for the twins, then opening her beautiful throat to take
it away. *These boots are made for walking, and that's
just what they'll do. One of these days these boots
are gonna walk all over you. Are you ready, boots? Start walkin'* . . .

Elvis's Twin Sister

Are you lonesome tonight? Do you miss me tonight?

Elvis is alive and she's female: Madonna

In the convent, y'all,
I tend the gardens,
watch things grow,
pray for the immortal soul
of rock'n'roll.

They call me
Sister Presley here.
The Reverend Mother
digs the way I move my hips
just like my brother

Gregorian chant
drifts out across the herbs,
Pascha nostrum immolatus est . . .
I wear a simple habit,
darkish hues,

a wimple with a novice-sewn
lace band, a rosary,
a chain of keys,
a pair of good and sturdy
blue suede shoes.

I think of it
as Graceland here,
a land of grace.
It puts my trademark slow lopsided smile
back on my face.

Lawdy.
I'm alive and well.
Long time since I walked
down Lonely Street
towards Heartbreak Hotel.

Pope Joan

After I learned to transubstantiate
unleavened bread
into the sacred host

and swung the burning frankincense
till blue-green snakes of smoke
coiled round the hem of my robe

and swayed through those fervent crowds,
high up in a papal chair,
blessing and blessing the air,

nearer to heaven
than cardinals, archbishops, bishops, priests,
being Vicar of Rome,

having made the Vatican my home,
like the best of men,
in nomine patris et filii et spiritus sancti, amen,

but twice as virtuous as them,
I came to believe
that I did not believe a word,

so I tell you now,
daughters or brides of the Lord,
that the closest I felt

to the power of God
was the sense of a hand
lifting me, flinging me down,

lifting me, flinging me down,
as my baby pushed out
from between my legs

where I lay in the road
in my miracle,
not a man or a pope at all.

Mrs Beast

These myths going round, these legends, fairy tales,
I'll put them straight; so when you stare
into my face – Helen's face, Cleopatra's,
Queen of Sheba's, Juliet's – then, deeper,
gaze into my eyes – Nefertiti's, Mona Lisa's,
Garbo's eyes – think again. The Little Mermaid slit
her shining, silver tail in two, rubbed salt
into that stinking wound, got up and walked,
in agony, in fishnet tights, stood up and smiled, waltzed,
all for a Prince, a pretty boy, a charming one
who'd dump her in the end, chuck her, throw her overboard.
I could have told her – look, love, I should know,
they're bastards when they're Princes.
What you want to do is find yourself a Beast. The sex

is better. Myself, I came to the House of the Beast
no longer a girl, knowing my own mind,
my own gold stashed in the bank,
my own black horse at the gates
ready to carry me off at one wrong word,
one false move, one dirty look.
But the Beast fell to his knees at the door
to kiss my glove with his mongrel lips – good –
showed by the tears in his bloodshot eyes
that he knew he was blessed – better –
didn't try to conceal his erection,
size of a mule's – best. And the Beast
watched me open, decant and quaff
a bottle of Chateau Margaux '54,
the year of my birth, before he lifted a paw.

I'll tell you more. Stripped of his muslin shirt
and his corduroys, he steamed in his pelt,
ugly as sin. He had the grunts, the groans, the yelps,
the breath of a goat. I had the language, girls.
The lady says, Do this. Harder. The lady says,
Do that. Faster. The lady says, That's not where I meant.
At last it all made sense. The pig in my bed
was *invited*. And if his snout and trotters fouled
my damask sheets, why, then, he'd wash them. Twice.
Meantime, here was his horrid leather tongue
to scour in between my toes. Here
were his hooked and yellowy claws to pick my nose,
if I wanted that. Or to scratch my back
till it bled. Here was his bullock's head
to sing off-key all night where I couldn't hear.
Here was a bit of him like a horse, a ram,
an ape, a wolf, a dog, a donkey, dragon, dinosaur.

Need I say more? On my Poker nights, the Beast
kept out of sight. We were a hard school, tough as fuck,
all of us beautiful and rich – the Woman
who Married a Minotaur, Goldilocks, the Bride
of the Bearded Lesbian, Frau Yellow Dwarf, et Moi.
I watched those wonderful women shuffle and deal –
Five and Seven Card Stud, Sidewinder, Hold 'Em, Draw –
I watched them bet and raise and call. One night,
a head-to-head between Frau Yellow Dwarf and Bearded's Bride
was over the biggest pot I'd seen in my puff.
The Frau had the Queen of Clubs on the baize
and Bearded the Queen of Spades. Final card. Queen each.
Frau Yellow raised. Bearded raised. Goldilock's eyes
were glued to the pot as though porridge bubbled there.
The Minotaur's wife lit a stinking cheroot. Me,
I noticed the Frau's hand shook as she placed her chips.

Bearded raised her a final time, then stared,
stared so hard you felt your dress would melt
if she blinked. I held my breath. Frau Yellow
swallowed hard, then called. Sure enough, Bearded flipped
her Aces over; diamonds, hearts, the pubic Ace of Spades.
And that was a lesson learnt by all of us –
the drop-dead gorgeous Bride of the Bearded Lesbian didn't bluff.

But behind each player stood a line of ghosts
unable to win. Eve. Ashputtel. Marilyn Monroe.
Rapunzel slashing wildly at her hair.
Bessie Smith unloved and down and out.
Bluebeard's wives, Henry VIII's, Snow White
cursing the day she left the seven dwarfs, Diana,
Princess of Wales. The sheepish Beast came in
with a tray of schnapps at the end of the game
and we stood for the toast – *Fay Wray* –
then tossed our fiery drinks to the back of our crimson throats.
Bad girls. Serious ladies. Mourning our dead.

So I was hard on the Beast, win or lose,
when I got upstairs, those tragic girls in my head,
turfing him out of bed; standing alone
on the balcony, the night so cold I could taste the stars
on the tip of my tongue. And I made a prayer –
thumbing my pearls, the tears of Mary, one by one,
like a rosary – words for the lost, the captive beautiful,
the wives, those less fortunate than we.
The moon was a hand mirror breathed on by a Queen.
My breath was an Isadora scarf for an elegant ghost.
I turned to go back inside. Bring me the Beast for the night.
Bring me the wine-cellar key. Let the less-loving one be me.

Demeter

Where I lived – winter and hard earth.
I sat in my cold stone room
choosing tough words, granite, flint,

to break the ice. My broken heart –
I tried that, but it skimmed,
flat, over the frozen lake.

She came from a long, long way,
but I saw her at last, walking,
my daughter, my girl, across the fields,

in bare feet, bringing all spring's flowers
to her mother's house. I swear
the air softened and warmed as she moved,

the blue sky smiling, none too soon,
with the small shy mouth of a new moon.

from Feminine Gospels

(2002)

The Long Queen

The Long Queen couldn't die.
Young when she bowed her head
for the cold weight of the crown, she'd looked
at the second son of the earl, the foreign prince,
the heir to the duke, the lord, the baronet, the count,
then taken Time for a husband. Long live the Queen.

What was she queen of? Women, girls,
spinsters and hags, matrons, wet nurses,
witches, widows, wives, mothers of all these.
Her word of law was in their bones, in the graft
of their hands, in the wild kicks of their dancing.
No girl born who wasn't the Long Queen's always child.

Unseen, she ruled and reigned; some said
in a castle, some said in a tower in the dark heart
of a wood, some said out and about in rags, disguised,
sorting the bad from the good. She sent her explorers away
in their creaking ships and was queen of more, of all the dead
when they lived if they did so female. All hail to the Queen.

What were her laws? *Childhood*: whether a girl
awoke from the bad dream of the worst, or another
swooned into memory, bereaved, bereft, or a third one
wrote it all down like a charge sheet, or the fourth never left,
scouring the markets and shops for her old books and toys –
no girl growing who wasn't the apple of the Long Queen's eye.

Blood: proof, in the Long Queen's colour,
royal red, of intent; the pain when a girl
first bled to be insignificant, no cause for complaint,
and this to be monthly, linked to the moon, till middle age
when the law would change. *Tears*: salt pearls, bright jewels
for the Long Queen's fingers to weigh as she counted their sorrow.

Childbirth: most to lie on the birthing beds,
push till the room screamed scarlet and children
bawled and slithered into their arms, sore flowers;
some to be godmother, aunt, teacher, teller of tall tales,
but all who were there to swear that the pain was worth it.
No mother bore daughter not named to honour the Queen.

And her pleasures were stories, true or false,
that came in the evening, drifting up on the air
to the high window she watched from, confession
or gossip, scandal or anecdote, secrets, her ear tuned
to the light music of girls, the drums of women, the faint strings
of the old. Long Queen. All her possessions for a moment of time.

The Map-Woman

A woman's skin was a map of the town
where she'd grown from a child.
When she went out, she covered it up
with a dress, with a shawl, with a hat,
with mitts or a muff, with leggings, trousers
or jeans, with an ankle-length coat, hooded
and fingertip-sleeved. But – birthmark, tattoo –
the A–Z street-map grew, a precise second skin,
broad if she binged, thin when she slimmed,
a precis of where to end or go back or begin.

Over her breast was the heart of the town,
from the Market Square to the Picture House
by way of St Mary's Church, a triangle
of alleys and streets and walks, her veins
like shadows below the lines of the map, the river
an artery snaking north to her neck. She knew
if you crossed the bridge at her nipple, took a left
and a right, you would come to the graves,
the grey-haired teachers of English and History,
the soldier boys, the Mayors and Councillors,

the beloved mothers and wives, the nuns and priests,
their bodies fading into the earth like old print
on a page. You could sit on a wooden bench
as a wedding pair ran, ringed, from the church,
confetti skittering over the marble stones,
the big bell hammering hail from the sky, and wonder
who you would marry and how and where and when
you would die; or find yourself in the coffee house
nearby, waiting for time to start, your tiny face
trapped in the window's bottle-thick glass like a fly.

And who might you see, short-cutting through
the Grove to the Square – that line there, the edge
of a fingernail pressed on her flesh – in the rain,
leaving your empty cup, to hurry on after
calling their name? When she showered, the map
gleamed on her skin, blue-black ink from a nib.
She knew you could scoot down Greengate Street,
huddling close to the High House, the sensible shops,
the Swan Hotel, till you came to the Picture House,
sat in the musty dark watching the Beatles

run for a train or Dustin Hoffman screaming
Elaine! Elaine! Elaine! or the spacemen in *2001*
floating to Strauss. She sponged, soaped, scrubbed;
the prison and hospital stamped on her back,
the park neat on her belly, her navel marking the spot
where the empty bandstand stood, the river again,
heading south, clear as an operation scar,
the war memorial facing the railway station
where trains sighed on the platform, pining
for Glasgow, London, Liverpool. She knew

you could stand on the railway bridge, waving
goodbye to strangers who stared as you vanished
into the belching steam, tasting future time
on the tip of your tongue. She knew you could run
the back way home – there it was on her thigh –
taking the southern road then cutting off to the left,
the big houses anchored behind their calm green lawns,
the jewels of conkers falling down at your feet,
then duck and dive down Nelson and Churchill
and Kipling and Milton Way until you were home.

She didn't live there now. She lived down south,
abroad, en route, up north, on a plane or train
or boat, on the road, in hotels, in the back of cabs,
on the phone; but the map was under her stockings,
under her gloves, under the soft silk scarf at her throat,
under her chiffon veil, a delicate braille. Her left knee
marked the grid of her own estate. When she knelt
she felt her father's house pressing into the bone,
heard in her head the looped soundtrack of then –
a tennis ball repeatedly thumping a wall,

an ice-cream van crying and hurrying on, a snarl
of children's shrieks from the overgrown land
where the houses ran out. The motorway groaned
just out of sight. She knew you could hitch
from Junction 13 and knew of a girl who had not
been seen since she did; had heard of a kid who'd run
across all six lanes for a dare before he was tossed
by a lorry into the air like a doll. But the motorway
was flowing away, was a roaring river of metal
and light, cheerio, au revoir, auf Wiedersehen, ciao.

She stared in the mirror as she got dressed,
both arms raised over her head, the roads
for east and west running from shoulder
to wrist, the fuzz of woodland or countryside under
each arm. Only her face was clear, her baby-blue eyes unsure
as they looked at themselves. But her body was certain,
an inch to the mile, knew every nook and cranny,
cul-de-sac, stile, back road, high road, low road,
one-way street of her past. There it all was, back

to front in the glass. She piled on linen, satin, silk,
leather, wool, perfume and mousse and went out.
She got in a limousine. The map perspired
under her clothes. She took a plane. The map seethed
on her flesh. She spoke in a foreign tongue.
The map translated everything back to herself.
She turned out the light and a lover's hands
caressed the map in the dark from north to south,
lost tourists wandering here and there, all fingers
and thumbs, as their map flapped in the breeze.

So one day, wondering where to go next,
she went back, drove a car for a night and a day,
till the town reappeared on her left, the stale cake
of the castle crumbled up on the hill; and she hired
a room with a view and soaked in the bath.
When it grew dark, she went out, thinking
she knew the place like the back of her hand,
but something was wrong. She got lost in arcades,
in streets with new names, in precincts
and walkways, and found that what was familiar

was only facade. Back in her hotel room, she stripped
and lay on the bed. As she slept, her skin sloughed
like a snake's, the skin of her legs like stockings, silvery,
sheer, like the long gloves of the skin of her arms,
the papery camisole from her chest a perfect match
for the tissuey socks of the skin of her feet. Her sleep
peeled her, lifted a honeymoon thong from her groin,
a delicate bra of skin from her breasts, and all of it
patterned A to Z; a small cross where her parents' skulls
grinned at the dark. Her new skin showed barely a mark.

She woke and spread out the map on the floor. What
was she looking for? Her skin was her own small ghost,
a shroud to be dead in, a newspaper for old news
to be read in, gift wrapping, litter, a suicide letter.
She left it there, dressed, checked out, got in the car.
As she drove, the town in the morning sun glittered
behind her. She ate up the miles. Her skin itched,
like a rash, like a slow burn, felt stretched, as though
it belonged to somebody else. Deep in the bone
old streets tunnelled and burrowed, hunting for home.

Beautiful

She was born from an egg,
a daughter of the gods,
divinely fair, a pearl, drop-dead
gorgeous, beautiful, a peach,
a child of grace, a stunner, in her face
the starlike sorrows of immortal eyes.
Who looked there, loved.

She won the heart
of every man she saw.
They stood in line, sighed,
knelt, beseeched, *Be Mine*.
She married one,
but every other mother's son
swore to be true to her
till death, enchanted
by the perfume of her breath,
her skin's celebrity.

So when she took a lover, fled,
was nowhere to be seen,
her side of the bed unslept in, cold,
the small coin of her wedding ring
left on the bedside table like a tip,
the wardrobe empty
of the drama of her clothes,
it was War.

A thousand ships –
on every one a thousand men,
each heaving at an oar,
each with her face
before his stinging eyes,
her name tattooed
upon the muscle of his arm,
a handkerchief she'd dropped once
for his lucky charm,
each seeing her as a local girl
made good, the girl next door,
a princess with the common touch,
queen of his heart, pin-up, superstar,
the heads of every coin he'd tossed,
the smile on every note he'd bet at cards –
bragged and shoved across a thousand miles of sea.

Meanwhile, lovely she lay high up
in a foreign castle's walls, clasped
in a hero's brawn, loved and loved
and loved again, her cries
like the bird of calamity's,
drifting down to the boys at the gates
who marched now to the syllables of her name.

Beauty is fame. Some said
she turned into a cloud
and floated home,
falling there like rain, or tears,
upon her husband's face.
Some said her lover woke
to find her gone,
his sword and clothes gone too,
before they sliced a last grin in his throat.

Some swore they saw her smuggled
on a boat dressed as a boy,
towed to a ship which slid away at dusk,
beckoned by a finger of the moon.
Some vowed that they were in the crowd
that saw her hung, stared up at her body
as it swung there on the creaking rope,
and noticed how the black silk of her dress
clung to her form, a stylish shroud.

Her maid, who loved her most,
refused to say one word
to anyone at any time or place,
would not describe
one aspect of her face
or tell one anecdote about her life and loves.

But lived alone
and kept a little bird inside a cage.

*

She never aged.
She sashayed up the river
in a golden barge,
her fit girls giggling at her jokes.
She'd tumbled from a rug at Caesar's feet,
seen him kneel to pick her up
and felt him want her as he did.
She had him gibbering in bed by twelve.

But now, she rolled her carpet on the sand,
put up her crimson tent, laid out
silver plate with grapes and honey, yogurt,
roasted songbirds, gleaming figs, soft wines,
and soaked herself in jasmine-scented milk.
She knew her man. She knew that when
he stood that night, ten times her strength,
inside the fragrant boudoir of her tent,
and saw her wrapped in satins like a gift,
his time would slow to nothing, zilch,
until his tongue could utter in her mouth.
She reached and pulled him down
to Alexandria, the warm muddy Nile.

Tough beauty. She played with him
at dice, rolled sixes in the dust,
cleaned up, slipped her gambling hand
into his pouch and took his gold, bit it,
Caesar's head between her teeth.
He crouched with lust. On her couch,
she lay above him, painted him,
her lipstick smeared on his mouth,
her powder blushing on his stubble,
the turquoise of her eyes over his lids.
She matched him glass for glass
in drinking games: sucked lemons, licked
at salt, swallowed something from a bottle
where a dead rat floated, gargled doubles
over trebles, downed a liquid fire in one,
lit a coffee bean in something else, blew it,
gulped, tipped chasers down her throat,
pints down her neck, and held her drink
until the big man slid beneath the table, wrecked.

She watched him hunt. He killed a stag.
She hacked the heart out, hid it,
dripping, in the apron of her dress.
She watched him exercise in arms.
His soldiers marched, eyes right, her way.
She let her shawl slip down to show
her shoulders, breasts, and every man
that night saw them again and prayed
her name. She waved him off to war,
then pulled on boy's clothes, crept
at dusk into his camp, his shadowed tent,
touched him, made him fuck her as a lad.
He had no choice, upped sticks,
downed tools, went back with her,
swooned on her flesh for months,
her fingers in his ears, her stories blethering
on his lips: of armies changing sides,
of cities lost forever in the sea, of snakes.

*

The camera loved her, close-up, back-lit,
adored the waxy pouting of her mouth,
her sleepy, startled gaze. She breathed
the script out in her little voice. They filmed her
famous, filmed her beautiful. Guys fell
in love, dames copied her. An athlete
licked the raindrops from her fingertips
to quench his thirst. She married him.
The US whooped.

They filmed her harder, harder, till her hair
was platinum, her teeth gems, her eyes
sapphires pressed by a banker's thumb.

She sang to camera one, gushed
at the greased-up lens, her skin investors' gold,
her fingernails mother-of-pearl, her voice
champagne to sip from her lips. A poet came,
found her wondrous to behold. She married him.
The whole world swooned.

Dumb beauty. She slept in an eye-mask, naked,
drugged, till the maid came, sponged
at her puffy face, painted the beauty on in khaki,
pinks, blues. Then it was coffee, pills, booze,
Frank on the record player, it was put on the mink,
get in the studio car. Somebody big was watching her –
white fur, mouth at the mike, under the lights. *Happy
Birthday to you. Happy Birthday, Mr President.*
The audience drooled.

They filmed on, deep, dumped what they couldn't use
on the cutting-room floor, filmed more, quiet please,
action, cut, quiet please, action, cut, quiet please
action, cut, till she couldn't die when she died,
couldn't get older, ill, couldn't stop saying the lines
or singing the tunes. The smoking cop who watched
as they zipped her into the body-bag noticed
her strong resemblance to herself, the dark roots
of her pubic hair.

*

Dead, she's elegant bone
in mud, ankles crossed,
knees clamped, hands clasped,
empty head. You know her name.

Plain women turned in the streets
where her shadow fell, under
her spell, swore that what she wore
they'd wear, coloured their hair.

The whole town came
to wave at her on her balcony,
to stare and stare and stare.
Her face was surely a star.

Beauty is fate. They gaped
as her bones danced
in a golden dress in the arms
of her wooden prince, gawped

as she posed alone
in front of the Taj Mahal,
betrayed, beautifully pale.
The cameras gibbered away.

Act like a fucking princess –
how they loved her,
the men from the press –
Give us a smile, cunt.

And her blue eyes widened
to take it all in: the flashbulbs,
the half-mast flags, the acres of flowers,
History's stinking breath in her face.

The Diet

The diet worked like a dream. No sugar,
salt, dairy, fat, protein, starch or alcohol.
By the end of week one, she was half a stone
shy of ten and shrinking, skipping breakfast,
lunch, dinner, thinner; a fortnight in, she was
eight stone; by the end of the month, she was skin
and bone.

She starved on, stayed in, stared in
the mirror, svelter, slimmer. The last apple
aged in the fruit bowl, untouched. The skimmed milk
soured in the fridge, unsupped. Her skeleton preened
under its tight flesh dress. She was all eyes,
all cheekbones, had guns for hips. Not a stitch
in the wardrobe fitted.

What passed her lips? Air,
water. She was Anorexia's true daughter, a slip
of a girl, a shadow, dwindling away. One day,
the width of a stick, she started to grow smaller –
child-sized, doll-sized, the height of a thimble.
She sat at her open window and the wind
blew her away.

Seed small, she was out and about,
looking for home. An empty beer bottle rolled
in the gutter. She crawled in, got drunk on the dregs,
started to sing, down, out, nobody's love. Tiny others
joined in. They raved all night. She woke alone,
head splitting, mouth dry, hungry and cold, and made
for the light.

She found she could fly on the wind,
could breathe, if it rained, underwater. That night,
she went to a hotel bar that she knew and floated into
the barman's eye. She slept for hours, left at dawn
in a blink, in a wink, drifted away on a breeze.
Minute, she could suit herself from here on in, go
where she pleased.

She stayed near people,
lay in the tent of a nostril like a germ, dwelled
in the caves of an ear. She lived in a tear, swam
clear, moved south to a mouth, kipped in the chap
of a lip. She loved flesh and blood, wallowed
in mud under fingernails, dossed in a fold of fat
on a waist.

But when she squatted the tip of a tongue,
she was gulped, swallowed, sent down the hatch
in a river of wine, bottoms up, cheers, fetched up
in a stomach just before lunch. She crouched
in the lining, hearing the avalanche munch of food,
then it was carrots, peas, courgettes, potatoes,
gravy and meat.

Then it was sweet. Then it was Stilton,
Roquefort, weisslacker-kase, gex; it was smoked salmon
with scrambled eggs, hot boiled ham, plum flan, frogs'
legs. She knew where she was all right, clambered
onto the greasy breast of a goose, opened wide, then
chomped and chewed and gorged; inside the Fat Woman now,
trying to get out.

Tall

Then, like a christening gift or a wish arriving
later in life, the woman had height, grew tall,
was taller daily.

Day one saw her rising at eight foot
bigger than any man. She knelt in the shower
as if she were praying for rain. Her clothes
would be curtains and eiderdowns, towels and rugs.

Out. Eye-high with street lamps, she took a walk
downtown. Somebody whooped. She stooped,
hands on both knees,

and stared at his scared face,
the red heart tattooed on his small chest. He turned
and fled like a boy.

On. A tree dangled an apple
at bite-height. She bit it. A traffic light stuttered
on red, went out. She lit it. Personal birds
sang on her ears. She whistled.

Further. Taller
as she went, she glanced into upper windows
in passing, saw lovers in the rented rooms
over shops, saw an old man long dead in a chair,
paused there, her breath on the glass.

She bowed herself into a bar, ordered a stiff drink.
It came on the rocks, on the house. A drunk
passed out or fainted. She pulled up a stool, sat
at the bar with her knees

                              under her chin, called
for another gin, a large one. She saw a face, high
in the mirror behind the top shelf. Herself.

Day two, she was hungover, all over, her head
in her hands in the hall, her feet at the top
of the stairs, more tall.

                              She needed a turret,
found one, day three, on the edge of town, moved in,
her head in the clouds now, showering in rain.

But pilgrims came –
small women with questions and worries, men
on stilts. She was thirty foot, growing, could see for miles.

So day six she upped sticks, horizon-bound
in seven-league boots. Local crowds swarmed
round her feet, chanting.

                              She cured no one. Grew.
The moon came closer at night, its scarred face
an old mirror. She slept outdoors, stretched
across empty fields or sand.

                              The stars trembled. Taller
was colder, aloner, no wiser. What could she see
up there? She told them what kind of weather
was heading their way –

dust storms over the Pyramids,
hurricanes over the USA, floods in the UK –
but by now the people were tiny

and far away, and she
was taller than Jupiter, Saturn, the Milky Way. Nothing
to see. She looked back and howled.

She stooped low
and caught their souls in her hands as they fell
from the burning towers.

History

She woke up old at last, alone,
bones in a bed, not a tooth
in her head, half dead, shuffled
and limped downstairs
in the rag of her nightdress,
smelling of pee.

Slurped tea, stared
at her hands – twigs, stained gloves –
wheezed and coughed, pulled on
the coat that hung from a hook
on the door, lay on the sofa,
dozed, snored.

She was History.
She'd seen them ease him down
from the Cross, his mother gasping
for breath, as though his death
was a difficult birth, the soldiers spitting,
spears in the earth;

been there
when the fishermen swore he was back
from the dead; seen the basilicas rise
in Jerusalem, Constantinople, Sicily; watched
for a hundred years as the air of Rome
turned into stone;

                    witnessed the wars,
the bloody crusades, knew them by date
and by name, Bannockburn, Passchendaele,
Babi Yar, Vietnam. She'd heard the last words
of the martyrs burnt at the stake, the murderers
hung by the neck,

                    seen up close
how the saint whistled and spat in the flames,
how the dictator strutting on stuttering film
blew out his brains, how the children waved
their little hands from the trains. She woke again,
cold, in the dark,

                    in the empty house.
Bricks through the window now, thieves
in the night. When they rang on her bell
there was nobody there; fresh graffiti sprayed
on her door, shit wrapped in a newspaper posted
onto the floor.

Anon

If she were here
she'd forget who she was,
it's been so long,
maybe a nurse, a nanny,
maybe a nun –
Anon.

A girl I met
was willing to bet
that she still lived on –
Anon –
but had packed it all in,
the best verb, the right noun,
for a life in the sun.

A woman I knew
kept her skull
on a shelf in a room –
Anon's –
and swore that one day
as she worked at her desk
it cleared its throat
as though it had something
to get off its chest.

But I know best –
how she passed on her pen
like a baton
down through the years,

with a hey nonny
hey nonny
hey nonny no –
Anon.

The Laughter of Stafford Girls' High

(for T.W.)

It was a girl in the Third Form, Carolann Clare,
who, bored with the lesson, the rivers of England –
Brathay, Coquet, Crake, Dee, Don, Goyt,
Rothay, Tyne, Swale, Tees, Wear, Wharfe . . .
had passed a note, which has never been found,
to the classmate in front, Emily Jane, a girl
who adored the teacher, Miss V. Dunn MA,
steadily squeaking her chalk on the board –
Allen, Clough, Duddon, Feugh, Greta, Hindburn,
Irwell, Kent, Leven, Lowther, Lune, Sprint . . .
but who furtively opened the folded note,
torn from the back of the King James Bible, read
what was scribbled there and laughed out loud.

It was a miserable, lowering winter's day. The girls
had been kept indoors at break – Wet Play
in the Hall – the windows tall and thin,
sad with rain like a long list of watery names –
Rawthey, Roeburn, Skirfare, Troutbeck, Wash . . .
likewise, the sound of the laugh of Emily Jane
was a liquid one, a gurgle, a ripple, a dribble,
a babble, a gargle, a plash, a splash of a laugh
like the sudden jackpot leap of a silver fish
in the purse of a pool. No fool, Emily Jane
clamped her turquoisey hand – her fountain pen leaked –
to her mouth; but the laugh was out, was at large,
was heard by the pupil twinned to her double desk –

Rosemary Beth – the brace on whose jiggly teeth
couldn't restrain the gulping giggle she gave
which caused Miss Dunn to spin round. *Perhaps,*
she said, *we can all share the joke?* But Emily Jane
had scrunched and dropped the note with the joke
to the floor and kicked it across to Jennifer Kay
who snorted and toed it to Marjorie May
who spluttered and heeled it backwards
to Jessica Kate. *Girls!* Miss Dunn's shrill voice
scraped Top G and only made matters worse.

Five minutes passed in a cauldron of noise.
No one could seem to stop. Each tried holding
her breath or thinking of death or pinching
her thigh, only to catch the eye of a pal,
a crimson, shaking, silent girl, and explode
through the nose in a cackling sneeze. *Thank you!*
Please! screeched Miss Dunn, clapping her hands
as though she applauded the choir they'd become,
a percussion of trills and whoops filling the room
like birds in a cage. But then came a triple rap
at the door and in stalked Miss Fife, Head of Maths,
whose cold equations of eyes scanned the desks
for a suitable scapegoat. *Stand up, Geraldine Ruth.*

Geraldine Ruth got to her feet, a pale girl, a girl
who looked, in the stale classroom light, like a sketch
for a girl, a first draft to be crumpled and crunched
and tossed away like a note. She cleared her throat,
raising her eyes, water and sky, to look at Miss Fife.
The girls who were there that day never forgot
how invisible crayons seemed to colour in
Geraldine Ruth, white face to puce, mousey hair
suddenly gifted with health and youth, and how –

as Miss Fife demanded what was the meaning of this –
her lips split from the closed bud of a kiss
to the daisy chain of a grin and how then she yodelled
a laugh with the full, open, blooming rose of her throat,

a flower of merriment. *What's the big joke?*
thundered Miss Fife as Miss Dunn began again
to clap, as gargling Geraldine Ruth collapsed
in a heap on her desk, as the rest of the class
hollered and hooted and howled. Miss Fife strode
on sharp heels to the blackboard, snatched up
a finger of chalk and jabbed and slashed out
a word. *SILENCE.* But the class next door,
Fourth Years learning the Beaufort scale with Miss Batt,
could hear the commotion. Miss Batt droned on –
*Nought, calm; one, light air; two, light breeze; three,
gentle . . . four, moderate . . . five, fresh . . . six, strong breeze;
seven, moderate gale . . .* Stephanie Fay started to laugh.

What's so amusing, Stephanie Fay? barked Miss Batt.
What's so amusing? echoed unwitting Miss Dunn
on the other side of the wall. *Precisely what's
so amusing?* chorused Miss Fife. The Fourth Years
shrieked with amazed delight and one wag,
Angela Joy, popped her head in the jaws of her desk
and bellowed, *What's so amusing? What's so
amusing?* into its musty yawn. The Third Form
guffawed afresh at the sound of the Fourth
and the noise of the two combined was heard
by the First Form, trying to get Shakespeare by heart
to the beat of the ruler of Mrs Mackay. *Don't look
at your books, look at me. After three. Friends,*

Romans, Countrymen . . . What's so amusing? rapped out
Mrs Mackay as the First Years chirruped
and trilled like baby birds in a nest at a worm;
but she heard for herself, appalled, the chaos
coming in waves through the wall and clipped
to the door. Uproar. And her Head of Lower School!
It was then that Mrs Mackay made mistake number one,
leaving her form on its own while she went to see
to the forms of Miss Batt and Miss Dunn. The moment
she'd gone, the room blossomed with paper planes,
ink bombs, whistles, snatches of song, and the class clown,
Caroline Joan – stood on her desk and took up
the speech where Mrs Mackay had left off – *Lend*

me your ears . . . just what the Second Form did
in the opposite room, reciting the Poets Laureate
for Miss Nadimbaba – *John Dryden, Thomas Shadwell,*
Nahum Tate, Nicholas Rowe, Laurence Eusden, Colley Cibber,
William Whitehead . . . but scattering titters and giggles
like noisy confetti on reaching Henry Pye as Caroline Joan
belted out Antony's speech in an Elvis style –
For Brutus, uh huh huh, is an honourable man.
Miss Nadimbaba, no fan of rock'n'roll, could scarcely
believe her ears, deducing at once that Mrs Mackay
was not with her class. She popped an anxious head
outside her door. Anarchy roared in her face
like a tropical wind. The corridor clock was at four.

The last bell rang. Although they would later regret it,
the teachers, taking their cue from wits' end Mrs Mackay,
allowed the chuckling, bright-eyed, mirthful girls
to go home, reprimand free, each woman privately glad
that the dark afternoon was over and done,

the chalky words rubbed away to dance as dust
on the air, the dates, the battles, the kings and queens,
the rivers and tributaries, poets, painters, playwrights,
politicos, popes . . . but they all agreed to make it quite clear
in tomorrow's Assembly that foolish behaviour –
even if only the once – wasn't admired or desired
at Stafford Girls' High. Above the school, the moon
was pinned like a monitor's badge to the sky.

Miss Dunn was the first to depart, wheeling
her bicycle through the gates, noticing how
the sky had cleared, a tidy diagram of the Plough
directly above. She liked it this cold, her breath
chiffoning out behind as she freewheeled home
down the hill, her mind emptying itself of geography,
of mountains and seas and deserts and forests
and capital cities. Her small terraced house looked,
she thought, like a sleeping face. She roused it
each evening, kisses of light on its cheeks
from her lamps, the small talk of cutlery, pots
and pans as she cooked, sweet silver steam caressing
the shy rooms of her home. Miss Dunn lived alone.

So did Miss Batt, in a flat on the edge of the park
near the school; though this evening Miss Fife
was coming for supper. The two were good friends
and Miss Fife liked to play on Miss Batt's small piano
after the meal and the slowly shared carafe of wine.
Music and Maths! Johann Sebastian Bach! Miss Batt,
an all-rounder, took out her marking – essays on Henry VIII
and his wives from the Fifth – while Miss Fife gave herself up
to Minuet in G. In between Catherine Howard

and Catherine Parr, Miss Batt glanced across at Fifi's
straight back as she played, each teacher conscious
of each woman's silently virtuous love. Nights like this,
twice a week, after school, for them both, seemed enough.

Mrs Mackay often gave Miss Nadimbaba a lift,
as they both, by coincidence, lived on Mulberry Drive –
Mrs Mackay with her husband of twenty-five grinding,
childless years; Miss Nadimbaba sharing a house
with her elderly aunt. Neither had ever invited
the other one in, although each would politely enquire
after her colleague's invisible half. Mrs Mackay
watched Miss Nadimbaba open her purple door and saw
a cat rubbing itself on her calf. She pulled away
from the kerb, worrying whether Mr Mackay would insist
on fish for his meal. Then he would do his crossword:
Mr Mackay calling out clues – *Kind of court for a bounder (8)* –
while she passed him *Roget*, *Brewer*, *Pears*, the *OED*.

The women teachers of England slept in their beds,
their shrewd or wise or sensible heads safe vessels
for Othello's jealousy, the Wife of Bath's warm laugh,
the phases of the moon, the country code;
for Roman numerals, Greek alphabets, French verbs;
for foreign currencies and Latin roots, for logarithms, tables,
quotes; the meanings of *currente calamo* and *fiat lux* and *stet*.
Miss Dunn dreamed of a freezing white terrain
where slowly moving elephants were made of ice.
Miss Nadimbaba dreamed she knelt to kiss Miss Barrett
on her couch and she, Miss Nadimbaba, was Browning
saying, *Beloved, be my wife* . . . and then a dog began to bark
and she woke up. Miss Batt dreamed of Miss Fife.

Morning Assembly – the world like Quink outside,
the teachers perched in a solemn row on the stage,
the Fifth and Sixth Forms clever and tall, Miss Fife
at the school piano, the Head herself, Doctor Bream,
at the stand – was a serious affair. *Jerusalem* hung
in the air till the last of Miss Fife's big chords
wobbled away. *Yesterday,* intoned Doctor Bream,
the Lower School behaved in a foolish way, sniggering
for most of the late afternoon. She glared at the girls
through her pince-nez and paused for dramatic effect.
But the First and Second and Third and Fourth Forms
started to laugh, each girl trying to swallow it down
till the sound was like distant thunder, the opening chord

of a storm. Miss Dunn and Miss Batt, Miss Nadimbaba
and Mrs Mackay leapt to their feet as one, grim-faced.
The Fifth Form hooted and howled. Miss Fife, oddly disturbed,
crashed down fistfuls of furious notes on the yellowing keys.
The Sixth Forms, upper and lower, shrieked. Señora Devizes,
sartorial, strict, slim, severe, teacher of Spanish,
stalked from the stage and stilettoed sharply down
to the back of the Hall to chastise the Fifth and Sixth.
¡Callaos! ¡Callaos! ¡Callaos! ¡Quedense! The whole school
guffawed; their pink young lungs flowering more
than they had for the hymn. ¡El clamor! The Hall was a zoo.
Snow began falling outside as though the clouds
were being slowly torn up like a rule book. *A good laugh,*

as the poet Ursula Fleur, who attended the school,
was to famously write, *is feasting on air.* The air that day
was chomped, chewed, bitten in two, pulled apart
like a wishbone, licked like a lollipop, sluiced and sucked.
Some of the girls were almost sick. Girls gulped or sipped
or slurped as they savoured the joke. What joke?

Nobody knew. A silly joy sparkled and fizzed. Tabitha Rose,
flower monitor for the day, wet herself, wailed, wept, ran
from the Hall, a small human shower of rain. The bell
for the start of lessons rang. Somehow the school
filed out in a raggedy line. The Head Girl, Josephine June,
scarlet-faced from killing herself, was in for a terrible time
with the Head. Snow iced the school like a giant cake.

No one on record recalls the words that were said,
but Josephine June was stripped of the Head Girl's badge
and sash and sent to the Sixth Form Common Room
to demand of the prefects how they could hope to grow to be
the finest of England's daughters and mothers and wives
after this morning's Assembly's abysmal affair?
But the crowd of girls gave a massive cheer, stamping
the floor with their feet in a rebel beat and Diana Kim,
Captain of Sports, jumped on a chair and declared
that if J.J. was no longer Head Girl then no one
would take her place. *All for one!* someone yelled. *And one
for all!* Diana Kim opened the window and jumped down
into the snow. With a shriek, Emmeline Belle jumped after her,

followed by cackling Anthea Meg, Melanie Hope, Andrea Lyn,
J.J. herself . . . It was Gillian Tess in the Fifth, being lectured
by tight-lipped Señora Devizes on how to behave, who glanced
from the first-floor window and noticed the Sixth Form
bouncing around in the snow like girls on the moon.
A snowball, the size of a netball, was creaking, rolling,
growing under their hands. *Look!* Girls at their windows gaped.
It grew from a ball to the size of a classroom globe. It grew
from a globe to the size of a huge balloon. Miss Dunn,
drumming the world's highest mountains into the heads

of the First Years – *Everest, K2, Kangchenjunga, Lhotse,*
   Makalu 1 . . .
flung open her window and breathed in the passionate cold
of the snow. A wild thought seeded itself in her head.

In later years, the size of the snowball rolled by the Sixth
grew like a legend. Some claimed that the Head, as it groaned
past her study, thought that there might have been an eclipse.
Ursula Fleur, in her prose poem, *Snow*, wrote that it took
the rest of the Michaelmas Term to melt. Miss Batt,
vacantly staring down as her class wrote out a list
of the monarchs of England – *Egbert, Ethelwulf, Ethelbald,*
Ethelbert, Ethelred, Alfred, Edward, Athelstan, Edmund,
Eadred, Eadwig, Edgar . . . noticed the snowball, huge and alone
on the hockey pitch, startlingly white in the pencilly grey
of the light, and thought of desire, of piano scales slowing,
slowing, breasts. She moaned aloud, forgetful of where
she was. Francesca Eve echoed the moan. The class roared.

But that night Miss Batt, while she cooked for Miss Fife,
who was opening the wine with a corkscrew
from last year's school trip to Siena and Florence,
felt herself naked, electric under her tartan skirt, twinset
and pearls; and later, Miss Fife at the piano, stroking
the first notes of Beethoven's 'Moonlight' Sonata, Miss Batt
came behind her, placing her inked and trembling hands
on her shoulders. A broken A minor chord stumbled
and died. Miss Fife said that Ludwig could only
have written this piece when he was in love. Miss Batt
pulled Miss Fife by the hair, turning her face around, hearing
her gasp, bending down, kissing her, kissing her, kissing her.
Essays on Cardinal Wolsey lay unmarked on the floor.

Across the hushed white park, down the slush of the hill,
Miss Dunn crouched on the floor of her sitting room
over a map of Tibet. The whisky glass in her nervous hand
clunked on her teeth, Talisker sheathing her tongue
in a heroine's warmth. She moved her finger slowly
over the map, the roof of the world. Her fingers walked to Nepal,
changing the mountain *Chomolungma* to *Sagarmatha*.
She sipped at her malt and thought about Mallory, lost
on Everest's slopes with his English Air, of how he'd wanted
to reach the summit *because it was there*. She wondered
whether he had. Nobody knew. She saw herself walking
the upper slopes with the Captain of Sports towards
the foetal shape of a sleeping man . . . She turned to the girl.

*

That Monday morning Doctor Bream, at her desk,
didn't yet know that the laughter of Stafford Girls' High
would not go away. But when she stood on the stage,
garbed in her Cambridge cap and gown, and told the school
to quietly stand and contemplate a fresh and serious start
to the week, and closed her eyes – the hush like an air balloon
tethered by ropes – a low and vulgar giggle yanked
at the silence. Doctor Bream kept her eyes clenched, hoping
that if she ignored it all would be well. Clumps of laughter
sprouted among the row upon row of girls. Doctor Bream,
determined and blind, started the morning's hymn. *I vow
to thee my country* . . . A flushed Miss Fife started to play.
All earthly things above . . . The rest of the staff joined in –

*entire and whole and perfect, the service of my love,
the love that asks no questions, the love that stands the test* . . .
But the girls were hysterical, watching the Head,
Queen Canute, singing against the tide of their mirth,

their shoals, their glittering laughter. She opened her eyes –
Clarice Maud Bream, MBE, DLitt – and saw, in the giggling sea,
one face which seemed to her to be worse, cheekier,
redder and louder, than all of the rest. Nigella Dawn
was fished by the Head from her seat and made to stand
on a chair on the stage. Laughter drained from the Hall. *This girl,*
boomed the Head, *will stand on this chair for as long as it takes
for the school to come to its senses. SILENCE!* The whole school
stood like a crowd waiting for news. The bell rang. Nobody

moved. Nobody made a sound. Minutes slinked away
as Nigella Dawn swayed on her creaky chair. The First Years
stared in shame at their shoes. The Head's tight smile
was a tick. *That,* she thought, in a phrase of her mother's,
has put the tin lid on that. A thin high whine, a kitten,
wind on a wire, came from behind. The school
seemed to hold its breath. Nigella Dawn shook on her chair.
The sound came again, louder. Doctor Bream looked to the staff.
Miss Batt had her head in her lap and was keening and rocking
backwards and forwards. The noise put the Head in mind
of a radio dial – *Luxembourg, Light, Hilversum, Welsh* –
as though the woman were trying to tune into herself. Miss Batt
flung her head back and laughed, laughed like a bride.

*

Mr and Mrs Mackay silently ate. She eyed him
boning his fish, slicing it down to the backbone,
sliding the skeleton out, fastidious, deft. She spied him
eat from the right of his plate to the left, ordered, precise.
She clenched herself for his voice. *A very nice dish
from the bottomless deep.* Bad words ran in her head like mice.
She wanted to write them down in the crossword lights.
14 Across: *F . . . 17 Down: F . . . . . . 2 Down: F . . . . . .*

Mr Mackay reached for the *OED*. She bit her lip. *A word
for one who is given to walking by night, not necessarily
in sleep*. She felt her heart flare in its dark cave, hungry, blind,
open its small beak. *Beginning with N*. Mrs Mackay
moved to the window and stared at the ravenous night. Later,

awake in the beached boat of the marital bed, Mrs Mackay
slid from between the sheets. Her spouse whistled and whined.
She dressed in sweater and slacks, in boots, in her old tweed coat,
and slipped from the house to a tut of the front-door snib.
Her breath swaggered away like a genie popped from a flask.
She looked for the moon, found it, arched high over the house,
a raised eyebrow of light, and started to walk. The streets
were empty, darkly sparkling under her feet, ribbons that tied
the sleeping town like a gift. A black cat glared from a wall.
Mrs Mackay walked and walked and walked, letting the night
sigh underneath her clothes, perfume her skin; letting it in,
the scented night – stone, starlight, tree-sleep, rat, owl.
A calm rhythm measured itself in her head. *Noctambulist*.

She walked for hours, till dawn's soft tip rubbed, smudged,
erased the dark. Back home, she stripped and washed
and dressed for school, moving about in the kitchen
till Mr Mackay appeared, requesting a four-minute egg
from a satisfied hen. She watched him slice off the top
with the side of his spoon, dip in his toast, savour the soft gold
of the yolk with his neat tongue. She thought of the girls,
how they'd laughed now for weeks. Panic nipped and salted
her eyes. And later that day, walking among the giggling desks
of the Third, she read Cleopatra's lament in a shaking voice
as tears shone on her cheeks: *Hast thou no care of me?
Shall I abide in this dull world, which in thy absence is
No better than a sty? O! see my women, the crown*

o' the earth doth melt. My lord! O! Withered is the garland
of the war, the soldier's pole is fall'n; young boys and girls
are level now with men; the odds is gone, and there is nothing
left remarkable beneath the visiting moon. Carolann Clare, trapped
in a breathless, crippling laugh, seriously thought she would die.
Mrs Mackay lay down her book and asked the girls to start
from the top and carry on reading the play round the class.
She closed her eyes and seemed to drift off at her desk. The voices of
girls shared Shakespeare, line by line, the clock
over the blackboard crumbling its minutes into the dusty air.
From the other side of the wall, light breezes of laughter came
and went. Further away, from the music room, the sound
of the orchestra hooted and sneered its way through Grieg.

Miss Batt, in the staffroom, marking the War of Jenkins' Ear
over and over again, put down her pen. Music reminded her
of Miss Fife. She lay her head on the table, dizzy with lust, longed
for the four o'clock bell, for home, for pasta and *vino rosso*,
for Fifi's body on hers in the single bed, for kisses that tasted
of jotters, of wine. She picked up an essay and read:
England went to war with Spain because a seaman, Robert
Jenkins, claimed that the Spanish thought him a smuggler
and cut off his ear. He showed the ear in the Commons
and public opinion forced the Government to declare war
on 23 October 1739 . . . Miss Batt cursed under her breath,
slashing a red tick with her pen. The music had stopped. Hilarity
squealed and screeched in its place down the corridor.

Miss Nadimbaba was teaching the poems of Yeats
to the Fifth when the girls in the orchestra laughed. She held
in her hands the poem which had made her a scribbler of verse
at twelve or thirteen. 'The Song' – she was sick of the laughter
at Stafford Girls' High – 'of Wandering Aengus'. She stared
at the girls in her class who were starting to shake. An epidemic,

that's what it was. It had gone on all term. It was now the air
that they breathed, teachers and girls: a giggling, sniggering,
gurgling, snickering atmosphere, a laughing gas that seeped
under doors, up corridors, into the gym, the chemistry lab,
the swimming pool, into Latin and Spanish and French and Greek,
into Needlework, History, Art, RK, PE, into cross-country runs,
into the silver apples of the moon, the golden apples of the sun.

Miss Dunn stood with her bike outside school after four,
scanning the silly, cackling girls for a face – Diana Kim's.
The Captain of Sports was tall, red-haired. Her green eyes
stared at Miss Dunn and Miss Dunn *knew*. This was a girl
who would scale a vertical wall of ice with her fingertips,
who would pitch a tent on the lip of a precipice, who would know
when the light was good, when the wind was bad, when snow
was powdery or hard. The girl had the stuff of heroines. Diana Kim
walked with the teacher, pushing her bicycle for her, hearing her
outline the journey, the great adventure, the climb to the Mother
of Earth. Something inside her opened and bloomed.
Miss Dunn was her destiny, fame, a strong hand pulling her
higher and higher into the far Tibetan clouds, into the sun.

*

Doctor Bream was well aware that something had to be done.
Laughter, it seemed, was on the curriculum. The girls
found everything funny, strange; howled or screamed
at the slightest thing. The Headmistress prowled the school,
listening at classroom doors. The new teacher, Mrs Munro,
was reading 'The Flaying of Marsyas' to the Third: *Help!*
Why are you stripping me from myself? The girls were in fits.
Mrs Munro's tight voice struggled on: *It was possible to count*
his throbbing organs and the chambers of his lungs. Shrieks

and squeals stabbed the air. Why? At what? Doctor Bream
snooped on. Miss Batt was teaching the First Form the names
of the nine major planets: *Mercury*, *Venus*, *Earth*, *Mars*,
Jupiter, *Saturn*, *Uranus* . . . Pandemonium hooted and whooped.

The grim Head passed down the corridor, hearing the Fifth Form
gargling its way through the Diet of Worms. She came
to the Honours Board, the names of the old girls written in gold –
Head Girls who had passed into legend, Captains of Sport
who had played the game, prize-winning girls, girls who'd gone on
to achieve great things. Members of Parliament! Blasts of laughter
belched from the playing fields. Doctor Bream walked to her room
and stood by her desk. Her certificates preened behind glass
in the wintery light. Silver medals and trophies and cups gleamed
in the cabinet. She went to the wall – the school photograph
glinted and glowed, each face like a fingertip; the pupils
straight-backed, straight-faced; the staff upright, strait-laced.
A warm giggle burbled outside. She flung open the door.

The empty corridor winked. She could hear
a distant piano practising 'Für Elise' . . . Señora Devizes
counting in Spanish in one of the rooms – *uno*, *dos*, *trés*,
cuatro, *cinco*, *séis*, *siete*, *ocho*, *nueve*, *diez*, *once*, *doce*,
trece, *catorce*, *quince*, *diez y séis*, *diez y siete*, *diez y ocho* . . .
a shrill whistle blowing outside . . . But then a burst of hysteria
came from the classroom above, rolled down the stairs,
exploded again in the classroom below. Mrs Mackay,
frantic, hoarse, could be heard pitching Portia's speech
over the hoots of the Fourth: *the quality of MERCY*
is not STRAINED. It droppeth as the gentle rain from HEAVEN
upon the place BENEATH . . . Cackles, like gunfire, crackled
and spat through the school. A cheer boomed from the Gym.

It went on thus – through every hymn or poem, catechism,
logarithm, sum, exam; in every classroom, drama room
to music room; on school trips to a factory or farm; from
First to Sixth Form, dunce to academic crème de la crème,
day in, day out; till, towards the end of the Hilary Term,
Doctor Bream called yet another meeting in the staffroom,
determined now to solve the problem of the laughter
of the girls once and for all. The staff filed in at 4.15 –
Miss Batt, Miss Fife, Miss Dunn, Mrs Munro, the sporty
Mrs Lee, Mrs Mackay, Miss Nadimbaba, the Heads of French
and Science – Miss Feaver, Mrs Kaye – Señora Devizes,
the tuneful Miss Aherne, the part-time drama teacher
Mrs Prendergast. The Head stood up and clapped her hands.

Miss Fife poured Earl Grey tea. Miss Dunn stood by the window,
staring out. Miss Batt burned at Miss Fife. Mrs Mackay
sat down and closed her eyes. Miss Nadimbaba churned
the closing couplet of a poem in her head. Miss Feaver
crossed her legs and smiled at Mrs Lee, who twirled
a squash racket between her rosy knees. *I think we all agree,*
said Doctor Bream, *that things are past the pale. The girls
are learning nothing. Discipline's completely gone
to pot. I'd like to hear from each of you in turn. Mrs Mackay?*
Mrs Mackay opened her eyes and sighed. And shook her head.
And then she started singing: *It was a lover and his lass,
with a hey, and a ho, and a hey nonino, that o'er
the green cornfield did pass, in the spring time,*

*the only pretty ring time, when birds do sing, hey ding
a ding, ding; sweet lovers love the spring.* A silence fell.
Miss Batt looked at Miss Fife and cleared her throat. *Miss Fife
and I are leaving at the end of term.* Miss Dunn at the window
turned. *I'm leaving then myself. To have a crack at Everest . . .*
The Head sank to a chair. Miss Nadimbaba stood. Then one by one

the staff resigned – to publish poetry, to live in Spain, to form
a tennis club, to run a restaurant in Nice, to tread the boards,
to sing in smoky clubs, to translate Ovid into current speech,
to study homeopathy. Doctor Bream was white with shock.
And what, she forced herself at last to say, *about the girls?*
Miss Batt, slowly undressing Fifi in the stockroom in her head,
winked at Miss Fife. She giggled girlishly. Miss Feaver laughed.

*

Small hours. The moon tracked Mrs Mackay as she reached the edge
of the sleeping town, houses dwindling to fields, the road
twisting up and away into the distant hills. She caught her mind
making anagrams – *grow heed, stab, rats* – and forced herself
to chant aloud as she walked. Hedgerow. Bats. Star. Her head
cleared. The town was below her now, dark and hunched,
a giant husband bunched in his sleep. Mrs Mackay climbed on,
higher and higher, keeping close to the ditch, till the road snaked
in a long S then levelled out into open countryside. *Shore,
love, steer, low, master, night loom, riven use, no.* Horse. Vole.
Trees. Owl. Stream. Moonlight. Universe. On. *Wed, loop, wand,
drib, tiles, pay thaw, god.* Dew. Pool. Dawn. Bird. Stile. Pathway.
Dog. She arrived at the fringe of a village as morning broke.

Miss Batt held Miss Fife in her arms at dawn, the small room
chaste with new light. Miss Fife began to talk in her sleep –
*The square of the hypotenuse is equal to the sum
of the squares of the other two sides.* Miss Batt slid down,
nuzzled her breastbone, her stomach, kissed down,
kissed down, down to the triangle. The tutting bedside clock
counted to five. They woke again at seven, stupid with love,
everything they knew – the brightest stars, Sirius, Canopus,
Alpha Centauri, Vega; the Roman Emperors, Claudius,

Nero, Galba, Otho, Vitellius; musical terms, *allegro, calando, crescendo, glissando*; mathematics, the value of pi, prime numbers, Cantor's infinities – only a jumble of words, a jumble of words. A long deep zero groaned from Miss Fife.

Miss Dunn took out her list and checked it again. Her class was sniggering its way through a test on Britain's largest lakes. She mouthed her list like a prayer: socks, mittens, shirt leggings, hat, face mask, goggles, harness, karabiners, ice screws, pitons, helmet, descender, ascender, loops, slings, ice axes, gaiters, crampons, boots, jacket, hood, trousers, water bottle, urine bottle, waste bags, sleeping bag, kit bag, head torch, batteries, tent, medical kit, maps, stove, butane, radio, fixing line, rope, cord, stoppers, wands, stakes and chocks and all of it twice. A sprinkle of giggles made her look up. *Pass your test to the girl on your left to be marked. The answers are: Lough Neagh, Lower Lough Erne, Loch Lomond, Loch Ness, Loch Awe, Upper Lough Erne* . . . Diana Kim climbed and climbed in her head.

Doctor Bream read through the letter to parents then signed her name at the end. The school was to close at the end of term until further notice. A dozen resignation notes from the staff lay on her desk. The Head put her head in her hands and wept. A local journalist lurked at the gates. Señora Devizes and Miss Nadimbaba entered the room to say that the girls were filing into the Hall for the Special Assembly. There was still no sign of Mrs Mackay. She looked at the shattered Head and Kipling sprang to Miss Nadimbaba's lips: *If you can force your heart and nerve and sinew to serve your turn long after they are gone* . . . Señora Devizes joined in: *Persiste aun no tengas fuerza, y solo te quede la voluntad que les dice: ¡Persiste!* The Head got to her feet and straightened her back.

And so, Doctor Bream summed up, *you girls have laughed this once great school into the ground. Señora Devizes plans to return to Spain.* Cries of *¡Olé! Miss Batt and Miss Fife have resigned.* Wolf whistles. *Mrs Prendergast is joining the Theatre Royale.*
A round of applause crashed on the boards like surf. The Head stared
at the laughing girls then turned and marched from the stage,
clipped up the polished corridor, banged through the double doors,
crunched down the gravel drive to the Staff Car Park and into her
car.
Elvis, shrieked Caroline Joan from the Hall, *has left the building.*
A cheer like an avalanche bounced off the roof. The Captain of
Sports
slipped from her seat and followed Miss Dunn. The girls burst
into song as their mute teachers walked from the stage. *Till we
have built Jerusalem in England's green and pleasant land.*

*

The empty school creaked and sighed, its desks the small coffins
of lessons, its blackboards the tombstones of learning. The books
in the Library stiffened and yellowed and curled. The portraits
of gone Headmistresses stared into space. The school groaned,
the tiles on its roofs falling off in its sleep, its windows as white
as chalk. The grass on the playing fields grew like grass
on a grave. Doctor Bream stared from her hospital window
over the fields. She could see the school bell in its tower glint
in the evening sun like a tear in an eye. She turned away. Postcards
and get-well messages from the staff were pinned to the wall.
She took down a picture of Everest from Miss Dunn: *We leave
Camp II tomorrow if the weather holds to climb the Corridor
to 21,000 feet. Both coping well with altitude. The Sherpas . . .*

Mrs Mackay walked through Glen Strathfarrar, mad, muttering, free; a filthy old pack on her back filled with scavenged loot – banana, bottle, blanket, balaclava, bread, blade, bible. She sat by a stream, filled her bottle and drank. She ate the crusts, the fruit. Kingfisher. Eagle. Heron. Red deer. Midge. The Glen darkened and cooled like History. Mrs Mackay lay in the heather under her blanket, mumbling lines from Lear: *As mad as the vex'd sea*; *singing aloud*; *crowned with rank fumitor and furrow weeds, with burdocks, hemlocks, nettles, cuckoo-flowers, darnel . . .* Syllables. Syllables. Sleep came suddenly, under the huge black, the chuckling clever stars. The Head at her window looked north to the clear night sky, to Pollux and Castor, Capella, Polaris, and wondered again what could have become of Mrs Mackay.

Rough lads from the town came up to the school to throw stones through the glass. Miss Batt and Miss Fife had moved to a city. They drank in a dark bar where women danced, cheek to cheek. Miss Batt loved Miss Fife till she sobbed and shook in her arms. Stray cats prowled through the classrooms, lunging at mice. Miss Fife dreamed that the school was a huge ship floating away from land, all hands lost, steered by a ghost, a woman whose face was the Head's, was Miss Nadimbaba's, then Mrs Mackay's, Mrs Lee's, Miss Feaver's, Miss Dunn's, Mrs Munro's, Mrs Kaye's, Miss Aherne's, Señora Devizes's . . . She woke in the darkness, a face over hers, a warm mouth kissing the gibberish from her lips. The school sank in her mind, a black wave taking it down as she gazed at the woman's face.

Miss Nadimbaba put down her pen and read through her poem. The palms of her hand felt light, that talented ache. She altered a verb and the line jumped on the page like a hooked fish. She needed
to type it up, but the poem was done. She was dying
to read it aloud to her aunt. She would open some wine.

In the hospital, a nurse brought warm milk and a pill to the Head,
who stared through the bars at the blackened hulk of the school.
By dawn, at John O'Groats, Mrs Mackay had finally run out of
     land.
She wrote her maiden name with a stick on the sand then walked
into the sea, steady at first, step by step, till the firm waves lifted her
under her arms and danced her away like a groom with a bride.
High above in the cold sky the seagulls, like schoolgirls, laughed.
Higher again, a teacher fell through the clouds with a girl in her
     arms.

A Dreaming Week

Not tonight, I'm dreaming
in the heart of the honeyed dark
in a boat of a bed in the attic room
in a house at the edge of the park
where the wind in the big old trees
creaks like an ark.

Not tomorrow, I'm dreaming
till dusk turns into dawn – *dust, must,*
most, moot, moon, mown, down –
with my hand on an open unread book,
a bird that's never flown . . . distantly
the birdsong of the telephone.

Not the following evening, I'm dreaming
in the monocle of the moon,
a sleeping *S* on the page of the bed
in the tome of a dim room, the rain
on the roof, rhyming there,
like the typed words of a poem.

Not the night after that, I'm dreaming
till the stars are blue in the face
printing the news of their old light
with the ink of space,
yards and yards of black silk night
to cover my sleeping face.

Not the next evening, I'm dreaming
in the crook of midnight's arm
like a lover held by another

safe from harm, like a child
stilled by a mother, soft and warm,
twelve golden faraway bells for a charm.

Not that night either, I'm dreaming
till the tides have come and gone
sighing over the frowning sand,
the whale's lonely song
scored on wave after wave of water
all the wet night long.

Not the last evening, I'm dreaming
under the stuttering clock,
under the covers, under closed eyes,
all colours fading to black,
the last of daylight hurrying
for a date with the glamorous dark.

The Light Gatherer

When you were small, your cupped palms
each held a candlesworth under the skin,
enough light to begin,

                and as you grew
light gathered in you, two clear raindrops
in your eyes,

         warm pearls, shy,
in the lobes of your ears, even always
the light of a smile after your tears.

Your kissed feet glowed in my one hand,
or I'd enter a room to see the corner you played in
lit like a stage set,

           the crown of your bowed head spotlit.
When language came, it glittered like a river,
silver, clever with fish,

         and you slept
with the whole moon held in your arms for a night light
where I knelt watching.

           Light gatherer. You fell from a star
into my lap, the soft lamp at the bedside
mirrored in you,

         and now you shine like a snowgirl,
a buttercup under a chin, the wide blue yonder
you squeal at and fly in,

         like a jewelled cave,
turquoise and diamond and gold, opening out
at the end of a tunnel of years.

Wish

But what if, in the clammy soil, her limbs
grew warmer, shifted, stirred, kicked off
the covering of earth, the drowsing corms,
the sly worms, what if her arms reached out
to grab the stone, the grooves of her dates
under her thumb, and pulled her up? I wish.
Her bare feet walk along the gravel path
between the graves, her shroud like washing
blown onto the grass, the petals of her wreath
kissed for a bride. Nobody died. Nobody
wept. Nobody slept who couldn't be woken
by the light. If I can only push open this heavy door
she'll be standing there in the sun, dirty, tired,
wondering why do I shout, why do I run.

North-West

(for Frances)

However it is we return to the water's edge
where the ferry grieves down by the Pier Head,
we do what we always did and get on board.
The city drifts out of reach. A huge silvery bird,
a kiss on the lip of the wind, follows our ship.
This is where we were young, the place no map
or heritage guide can reveal. Only an X on a wave
marks the spot, the flowers of litter, a grave
for our ruined loves, unborn children, ghosts.
We look back at the skyline, wondering what we lost
in the hidden streets, in the rented rooms,
no more than punters now in a tourist boom.
Above our heads the gulls cry *yeah yeah yeah*.
Frets of light on the river. Tearful air.

Death and the Moon

(for Catherine Marcangeli)

The moon is nearer than where death took you
at the end of the old year. Cold as cash
in the sky's dark pocket, its hard old face
is gold as a mask tonight. I break the ice
over the fish in my frozen pond, look up
as the ghosts of my wordless breath reach
for the stars. If I stood on the tip of my toes
and stretched, I could touch the edge of the moon.

I stooped at the lip of your open grave
to gather a fistful of earth, hard rain,
tough confetti, and tossed it down. It stuttered
like morse on the wood over your eyes, your tongue,
your soundless ears. Then as I slept my living sleep
the ground gulped you, swallowed you whole,
and though I was there when you died,
in the red cave of your widow's unbearable cry,

and measured the space between last words
and silence, I cannot say where you are. Unreachable
by prayer, even if poems are prayers. Unseeable
in the air, even if souls are stars. I turn
to the house, its windows tender with light, the moon,
surely, only as far again as the roof. The goldfish
are tongues in the water's mouth. The black night
is huge, mute, and you are further forever than that.

Index of Titles

Index of First Lines